◗ Plough Quarterly

BREAKING GROUND FOR A RENEWED WORLD

Summer 2015, Number 5

Artists: Marc Chagall, Egon Schiele, Lisa Toth, Carl Larsson,
Ben Shahn, Jason Landsel, Mikalojus Konstantinas Čiurlionis,
Paul Klee, Antonello da Messina

About the cover: *When the Harara family's children returned to their bombed home in Gaza in 2014, they found undetonated shells. They scraped out the explosives and used them as flowerpots.*
Photograph by Kyrre Lien.

WWW.PLOUGH.COM

Plough Quarterly

BREAKING GROUND FOR A RENEWED WORLD

www.plough.com

Plough Quarterly features original stories, ideas, and culture to inspire everyday faith and action. Starting from the conviction that the teachings and example of Jesus can transform and renew our world, we aim to apply them to all aspects of life, seeking common ground with all people of goodwill regardless of creed. The goal of *Plough Quarterly* is to build a living network of readers, contributors, and practitioners so that, in the words of Hebrews, we may "spur one another on toward love and good deeds."

Plough Quarterly is published by Plough, the publishing house of the Bruderhof, an international movement of Christian communities whose members are called to follow Jesus together in the spirit of the Sermon on the Mount and of the first church in Jerusalem, sharing all talents, income, and possessions (Acts 2 and 4). Bruderhof communities, which include both families and single people from a wide range of backgrounds, are located in the United States, England, Germany, Australia, and Paraguay. Visitors are welcome at any time. To learn more about the Bruderhof's faith, history, and daily life, or to find a community near you to arrange a visit, go to *www.bruderhof.com*.

We include contributions in the *Plough Quarterly* which we believe are worthy of our readers' consideration, whether or not we fully agree with them. Views expressed by contributors are their own and do not necessarily reflect the editorial position of Plough or of the Bruderhof communities.

Editors: Peter Mommsen, Sam Hine, Maureen Swinger. Art director: Emily Alexander. Online editor: Erna Albertz. Contributing editors: Veery Huleatt, Chungyon Won, Helen Huleatt, Charles Moore. Founding Editor: Eberhard Arnold (1883–1935)

Plough Quarterly No. 5: Peacemakers
Published by Plough Publishing House, ISBN 978-0-87486-691-9
Copyright © 2015 by Plough Publishing House. All rights reserved.

All Scripture quotations are taken from the New Revised Standard Version unless otherwise noted.

Front cover: photograph by Kyrre Lien, www.kyrrelien.com. Inside front cover: Marc Chagall, *Prayer*, image from Scala / Art Resource, New York copyright © 2015 / Artists Rights Society (ARS), New York. Back cover art: Dora Holzhandler, *Sabbath Candles*, 2007, RONA Gallery, London, UK / Bridgeman Images.

Poem on page 23 reprinted from *Scavenger Loop: Poems* by David Baker, copyright © 2015 David Baker, with permission of the publisher, W. W. Norton & Company, Inc. All rights reserved. Reading from Dietrich Bonhoeffer on page 47 is from *The Cost of Discipleship*, SCM Translation, copyright © 1959 SCM Press. Used by permission of Hymns Ancient & Modern Ltd.

Editorial Office	*Subscriber Services*	*United Kingdom*	*Australia*
PO Box 398	PO Box 345	Brightling Road	4188 Gwydir Highway
Walden, NY 12586	Congers, NY 10920-0345	Robertsbridge	Elsmore, NSW
T: 845.572.3455	T: 800.521.8011	TN32 5DR	2360 Australia
info@plough.com	*subscriptions@plough.com*	T: +44(0)1580.883.344	T: +61(0)2.6723.2213

Plough Quarterly (ISSN 2372-2584) is published quarterly by Plough Publishing House, PO Box 398, Walden, NY 12586.
Individual subscription $32 per year in the United States; Canada add $8, other countries add $16.
Application to mail at periodicals postage pricing is pending at Walden, NY, and additional mailing offices.
POSTMASTER: Send address changes to *Plough Quarterly*, PO Box 345, Congers, NY 10920-0345.

Dear Reader,

Peacemaking, like a Bach sonata or a Philly cheese steak, is uncontroversially good. Everyone is for it; nobody (crazies aside) is against it. Other activities to which Christians are called can easily arouse opposition: pressing for justice, seeking purity of heart, speaking the plain truth, or living in voluntary poverty. But who will hate a peacemaker? In our live-and-let-live, so-long-as-it-doesn't-hurt-anyone culture, peace seems like something we can all agree on.

And so it should be – as long as we remember what peace asks of us. The contributors to this issue of *Plough Quarterly* show us what peacemaking looks like. Of course, they can only offer us views from this or that particular angle – the topic is too big for tidy theories. Still, a rich and challenging picture emerges. Peacemaking, these stories and reflections show, is a more ambitious undertaking, and a riskier one, than we may have imagined.

Yet peacemakers are urgently needed, just as they always have been. Today we must wage peace where thousands of children are being murdered by militias or forced to fight as soldiers. We are to be peacemakers in divided cities from Paris to Baltimore, peacemakers in a culture with little tolerance for Christian witness, and peacemakers in churches riven by ideological fights and petty grudges. We are to make and keep peace with our spouses, and with ourselves.

"Blessed are the peacemakers" turns out to be no warm and fuzzy slogan, then. It's a promise of an upended world. And it's a calling for which we must be willing to chance everything.

How should we pursue peace? The contributors here don't all agree with each other, nor will you with all of them. Our goal is to seek the truth together. We look forward to hearing from you.

Warm greetings,

Peter

Peter Mommsen
Editor

Photograph "Plowing rich prairie soil with tractor, South Dakota" from the Robert N. Dennis collection of stereoscopic views, Wikimedia Commons (public domain).

No Prosperity Gospel

On Kwon Jeong-saeng's "The Church I Dreamed Of," Autumn 2014: This article could have been written for the churches in the USA. We have come so far from the simplicity of worship without complication or reservation. Money has become all-consuming, and even the gospel has been perverted to encourage us to give with the promise of returned wealth – what a lie.

Trisha Freitag

Finding God in Creation

On Claudio Oliver's "Becoming a Rooted Church," Spring 2015: I live in the United States, but part of my family lives in Brazil, which holds a special place in my heart. Now I'm seventy-five, and I realize that it took me much longer to hear the Message that you have heard. We live here with an organic garden and a tribe of abandoned dogs and cats. We feel God's presence as we simply focus on the animals and our visitors, trying to keep our minds open. God bless you.

Patricia Silva

John Muir's Bible

On Calvin B. DeWitt's "The Psalmic Soundtrack of John Muir," Spring 2015: Thanks, Dr. DeWitt! In college I studied the religion of John Muir. This article, with its copious quotes, was not only a reminder of that semester but also a worshipful experience.

Dean Van Farowe

Can Wars Be Just?

On Ron Sider's "Does ISIS Prove Nonviolence Wrong?", Winter 2015: It's hard for me to take the Just War theory seriously. Show me one Christian denomination that is capable of applying it. It may be a great discussion topic for theologians, but unless there is a plan of implementation it's not serious. Can you imagine a church saying, "This is not a just war by our criteria; therefore we call on all members to refrain from any form of participation in it, including our active military members, since participating in an unjust war is tantamount to committing murder?"

Steve Dintaman

We need to acknowledge right off the bat that the empire (the USA and its allies) has actively supported the arming and training of extremist (Wahhabi) Muslims since 1979. This strategy began in Afghanistan and has been used since in other countries. To stop ISIS, we must confront the possibility that it is the US government and its allies that are at the root of terror. No matter what the cause of violence, Jesus-followers betray the radical core of the gospel when they take on the task of solving these problems within imperial categories of thought.

Berry Friesen

Steering the Plough

On Plough's Spring 2015 issue: You asked for feedback on the magazine's design. I noticed that in the last issue there seemed to be an emphasis on space and graphics, or was it bigger print size? [Ed.: Yes.] My concern is that *Plough* is not a pretty coffee table magazine, but a magazine that offers spiritual sustenance. The reader needs articles of a reasonable length with religious, theological, and inspirational substance. Small articles have their place, but we need solid food for thought as well. Thanks for a truly unique magazine.

Bob Pounder

This new *Plough Quarterly* is simply amazing. There's an authentic ecumenical spirit that flickers through the pages.

Katie Thamer Treherne

As a subscriber in Cuba, I agree that *Plough* truly is "much more than just a magazine." Never lose the Christocentric voice that you represent.

Rafael Godínez Soler

We welcome letters to the editor. Letters and web comments may be edited for length and clarity, and may be published in any medium. Letters should be sent with the writer's name and address to letters@plough.com.

BY MAUREEN SWINGER

Crossing a New Rubicon

In January 2010, a 7.0 magnitude earthquake rocked Port-au-Prince, Haiti. Thousands were killed, and almost a million people lost their homes and livelihoods in the space of a few minutes. Marine Corps veterans William McNulty and Jake Wood weren't affiliated with any aid network, but in the first critical hours after the disaster they saw a gap that wasn't being filled fast enough. They teamed up with six other veterans and first responders and traveled to Haiti, carrying medical supplies donated by friends and family. The scale of the catastrophe called to mind a combat zone, and they found that their battle training now stood them in good stead as they ventured into unstable, overlooked areas to rescue survivors, provide triage, and dispense food.

This first spontaneous deployment proved contagious, as other veterans teamed up to intervene in disasters closer to home: Hurricane Sandy in 2012, the devastating Midwestern tornadoes, and more recently, flooding in rural West Virginia. As the program expanded, it was dubbed Team Rubicon, connoting an expeditionary force that doesn't turn back.

Five years after the team's first venture, one thing has become clear in their minds: those at the receiving end of their aid are not the only ones to benefit.

Veteran Harry Golden, who served in the Navy and National Guard, was leading a platoon in Ramadi, Iraq, when it came under heavy fire. He was transported home with a critical spinal cord injury. Now he speaks for many who are finding renewal in an unexpected chance to do what they do best:

> I had spent the past seven years being pissed off at the world and drinking, like many of us do. That wasn't getting me anywhere. I was aware of Team Rubicon, but wasn't certain they would take me given my disabilities. . . . It's good to feel needed again. Disaster is chaos, and what us combat veterans do best is chaos management. This is war: this is full-on combat on the front lines – without the violence.
>
> As a result of this mission, people are starting to understand us. I've found that I still have something to give. There's still something there. I'm here helping people, but as a result, it's saving my own life. ➤

In the wake of the recent 7.8 magnitude earthquake in Nepal, Team Rubicon has deployed a team to Kathmandu. Follow or support Operation Tenzing and other Team Rubicon actions at www.teamrubiconusa.org.

Passing on the Gift

This proud alpaca owner participates in a Heifer International project in the uplands of Bolivia.

American farmer Dan West knew giving refugees a cup of milk a day was not enough. What if he could give them a cow instead? Seventy years after "Heifer for Relief" shipped its first cows to impoverished villagers in post-war Europe, West's "teach a man to fish" approach has helped lift more than twenty million families around the world out of hunger and poverty.

Today, Heifer International oversees sustainable development projects on five continents, improving education, animal management, accountability, and sanitation. But providing livestock remains the core of its work. From rabbits, goats, and hogs to cows, llamas, and camels, the gift is tailored to the specific village's climate and culture. Milk, wool, and meat, in addition to combatting hunger, provide an income with which a family can send a child to school or improve their home.

Part of the deal is "passing on the gift," Heifer's long-standing policy that the recipient must give away the offspring of that animal to another person in need. In this way, families build community in a cycle of positive change.

On average, "passing on the gift" carries on for at least nine generations of animals, and in some places, twenty-two generations can be traced!

Since most animals are now sourced locally in the countries being served, the original Heifer Ranch in Arkansas has become a place where privileged children can learn about the root causes of hunger and poverty, spending a night on dirt floors in the "Global Village" after a frugal meal.

Find out how you can give "a hand up, not a handout" at *www.heifer.org.*

Bearing Witness

Who are today's martyrs? Beginning with the death of Stephen around AD 34, the church has commemorated those who suffered for their faith in Christ. In the Anabaptist tradition, especially, stories of martyrs have shaped church communities through books such as the *Hutterian Chronicle* (ca. 1665) and Thieleman von Braght's *Martyrs' Mirror* (1685).

The stories of more recent Christian witnesses, however, are often unknown. In response, the Bearing Witness Stories Project – an effort to collect testimonies of Anabaptist believers who suffered for their faith – seeks to remind us what costly discipleship looks like. The project aims to encourage faithfulness to the way of Jesus by building on the spiritual legacy of *Martyrs' Mirror,* says John Roth, professor of history and director of Goshen College's Institute for the Study of Global Anabaptism, which initiated the project. Recently featured stories include a Congolese pastor who forgave the armed men who forced him to dig his own grave, a Ukrainian Mennonite Brethren family dispersed to Soviet labor camps, and a missionary in China forced into hiding during World War II. People throughout the world are invited to share stories on the Bearing Witness Story Project website, *www.martyrstories.org.*

Featured Books from Plough

Seeking Peace: Notes and Conversations along the Way

By Johann Christoph Arnold. Where can we find peace of heart and mind – with ourselves, with others, and with God? There is a peace greater than self-fulfillment, Arnold writes, a peace greater than nations no longer at war. But it will demand courage, vision, and commitment. *Seeking Peace* explores many facets of human-kind's ageless search for peace. It plumbs a wealth of spiritual traditions and draws on the wisdom of some exceptional (and some very ordinary) people who have found peace in surprising places. (See excerpt on page 19.)

> "*Seeking Peace* is a tough, transcendent envisioning of peace. Arnold writes in the tradition of the Berrigans, Simone Weil, and Thomas Merton."—Jonathan Kozol

Six Months to Live

By Daniel Hallock. A month before his wedding, twenty-two-year-old Matt Gauger was diagnosed with lymphoma. This is the story of how Matt and his family and friends struggled to accept his suffering and imminent death, and how it changed each of them. Hallock draws the reader into the experience from every perspective – in the words of Matt's wife, parents, brother, doctor, pastor, friends, and colleagues – to show how our lives can take on new depth of meaning when we realize that our days are numbered and face (rather than avoid) life's most important questions.

> "Deep, fascinating, theologically rich. . . ." —*Christianity Today*

> "Powerful. . . . It is rare to be invited on such an intimate journey." —N. Gordon Cosby

The Awakening: One Man's Battle with Darkness

By Friedrich Zuendel. When a pastor agrees to counsel a tormented woman in his congregation, all hell breaks loose. But that is only the beginning of the drama that ensues. *The Awakening* provides a rare glimpse into how forces of good and evil play themselves out in the lives of the most ordinary people, and reminds us that those forces still surround us today, whether we are awake to them or not.

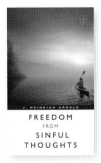

> "Anyone who has doubts about spiritual warfare must read this book."—Tony Campolo

> "A riveting testimony to the power of prayer and repentance."—*Charisma Magazine*

Freedom from Sinful Thoughts

By J. Heinrich Arnold. We don't talk about them, but all of us have them – private jealousies, resentments, fantasies, and temptations. For over four decades, Arnold's sensitive wisdom has helped thousands of readers battle these unwanted thoughts. Drawing on the words of Jesus and on his own experience as a pastor, Arnold guides the reader from frustration, guilt, and self-doubt to single-minded freedom and peace in Christ.

> "Arnold's deep-rootedness in Christ makes him a very wise, a very safe, and a very challenging guide." —Henri J. M. Nouwen

www.plough.com
Free access to dozens of e-books for subscribers

Jesus Abbey

AN INTERVIEW WITH BEN TORREY

RECONCILING A DIVIDED KOREA

The summer of 2000 was exceptionally hot and humid in Korea, and I was sweating as I climbed the steep mountain path to Jesus Abbey, a Christian community founded in 1965 by the American missionaries Archer and Jane Torrey near the northeastern city of Taebaek. My recent graduation from university, which should have been a triumph, had left a sour taste in my mouth. At twenty-six, I was sick of the competition and academic pressure that squeezed any joy out of learning. And the student protests in which I'd enthusiastically joined proved just as unsatisfying – once the demonstrations were over, my circle of friends in the movement drifted apart for lack of a common purpose. My conscience was burdened, and I was thirsting to find peace.

When a friend told me about a community on the mountain where life was shared in Christian comradeship, I hurried to see for myself. Rounding a bend in the trail, I saw sturdy-looking traditional houses built against a rocky slope. People came out to meet me, and it was as if peace was reaching toward me through their welcoming faces. I was a stranger, yet I sensed that in this place I could voice my questions, my fears, my hopes. In the days that followed, encircled by the grandeur and silence of the mountains, I began to experience a change of life. Fifteen years later, I'm still grateful.

This year at Pentecost, Jesus Abbey will be celebrating its fifty-year jubilee. On behalf of *Plough* I have used this occasion to interview Ben Torrey, Jane and Archer's son, who has served Jesus Abbey with his wife Liz since 2005.

Won Maroo

When your father founded Jesus Abbey fifty years ago, he said he wanted it to be "a laboratory of Christian life." What did he mean?

Actually he wanted it to be three laboratories. The first lab has to do with our individual relationship with God, focusing on prayer: do we trust God to guide us and provide for our needs? The second lab concerns our relationship to one another in Christ: are we able to live together in love? The third lab addresses the relationship of the Christian community with the world: Are we concerned with society's problems? Are we the hands and feet of Jesus in the world, expressing his love in practical ways?

Let's talk about the second lab – relationships in community. What does that look like at Jesus Abbey?

Koinonia, or unity, is a gift of the Holy Spirit. Recently we have been thinking that we need to love more – we are aware how far short we fall. The most important thing is to keep praying that the Holy Spirit works among us to soften hearts.

We have tried to develop a culture that makes it easy to ask forgiveness. When someone apologizes, we respond by saying, "Shalom," meaning, "You are forgiven." Every now and then, people do this if they've made a mistake

Photographs courtesy of the Jesus Abbey

that impacts others. For example, when I gave a lecture last week, the sister who had prepared the slides botched the job because she was in a rush. At the end of the lecture, she stood up and apologized. There was a spontaneous response of "Shalom."

We take Jesus' words seriously that "when you are offering your gift at the altar, if you remember that your brother or sister has something against you, leave your gift there before the altar and go; first be reconciled to your brother or sister, and then come and offer your gift" (Matt. 5:23–24). If there is a problem between two people, they are encouraged to seek forgiveness directly and be reconciled before coming to communion. Every Sunday during the celebration of the Eucharist we have a time of public confession and reconciliation. We wait in silence for a few minutes to give opportunity for people to confess sins that may be troubling them. Nobody is forced to do this. When someone is moved to do so, we all respond with "Shalom." Last Sunday two of our teenagers publicly asked for forgiveness.

Is it possible for the same kind of reconciliation to take place on a broader scale – for instance, between South and North Korea?

Yes, as we've seen on a small scale here. Three Seas Ranch is the name of a property that Jesus Abbey has been leasing since 1975 to raise livestock. Its name stems from the fact that it is located where Korea's three watersheds meet; rain falling here may find its way into the Han River flowing west, the Fifty Creeks flowing into the East Sea, or the Nakdong River flowing south.

One of my parents' friends pointed out that there should be a fourth river flowing from this place: the River of Life streaming into North Korea. So the Fourth River Project came into being. Its purpose is to equip South Koreans to share Jesus' living water with our brothers and sisters in the North. We believe doors will open someday. When that great moment comes, the love of Christ must be brought in humility to our brothers and sisters in the North, in a way they will understand.

You've started this mission right at Jesus Abbey's Three Seas Ranch by bringing North Korean defectors together with South Koreans. What happens when the two groups spend time together?

We have held these labor schools for the last eight summers. Through these conferences, our young people develop ongoing friendships and learn to trust one another. The North Koreans share their perspectives, which is important for them, because they usually try to just fit into society and deny their roots, knowing that most people in the South don't want to hear about it.

We spend mornings doing physical work – cutting trees, clearing pastureland, or cleaning the barns. Often the North Korean defectors are the ones who demonstrate how to work. One year as we felled trees with hand saws, a twenty-three-year-old woman from the North was sawing expertly, working her way rapidly up the hill; she had been doing this type of work since she was fourteen. It was affirming for her that her skill was appreciated here in South Korea. She became a role model in the labor school.

You've visited North Korea to help distribute humanitarian aid. What is it like?

I met many good people and saw much beauty while traveling through North Korea. I also saw a society trapped in great deception. I felt like I was operating inside a vast cult much of the time. I realized that people in the North have as little understanding of the vast gulf as those in the South. One of my colleagues praised my concern about preparing for reunification, but said my efforts were unnecessary: "We speak the same language. We are one culture. We will unite without difficulty." That is an assumption I've seen in both the North and South. Unfortunately, it is far from the truth.

What special challenges do you see in bringing the gospel to the North?

We need to develop a spirit of community and of cooperation. That means coming alongside North Koreans as brothers and sisters rather than as "experts" bringing something that we have and that they need. We must go in deep humility and understand that this is a cross-cultural work – a task that will require much preparation.

Yet beyond these challenges, the greatest need is for unity within the church. If the present church, with all its competition and corruption, goes into the North, I fear people will be prevented from meeting Jesus Christ. And the materialism of South Korea could be devastating to the North.

If the church's division is such an obstacle, how can it be overcome?

To seek true unity with God and with our brothers and sisters, we need to be humble, forgive others, and love each other. Then God will work among us. Only the Holy Spirit can bring repentance, forgiveness, healing, and true unity. If we experience the baptism of the Holy Spirit, we will be empowered for the task Christ asks of us – and that includes serving the people of North Korea and preparing for the reunification of Korea. I believe that this can happen, through the work of the Holy Spirit poured out upon this nation. ➤

Interview by Won Maroo on April 21, 2015.

THE FOUNDERS: ARCHER AND JANE TORREY

Archer Torrey was born in China in 1918 to missionary parents. After working as a commercial sailor during World War II (he was a conscientious objector), in 1957 he was invited to Seoul to revive an Anglican seminary. Soon Archer and his wife Jane were dreaming of a place in South Korea where people could find Jesus and experience God's justice. So in 1965, with their son Ben and a few volunteers, they moved to the Taebaek Mountains to start building what became Jesus Abbey.

A stream of people soon poured through the community, and hasn't stopped since. Some join as members, but most stay for shorter periods of communal work and worship. The Torreys tirelessly served these guests until Archer's death in 2002 and Jane's ten years later. About seventy people, including children, live at Jesus Abbey now, and about five thousand visit yearly. Anyone wishing to participate in Jesus Abbey's Jubilee celebration in North America can join the weekend at Montrose Bible Conference (Pennsylvania), September 25–27, 2015. Find out about the Jesus Abbey's reconciliation work at *www.thefourthriver.org.*

Painting by Ian Mow

Lessons *from a* Village Cow

Smooth, creamy yoghurt, whipped and cool, with a bit of sugar. Where does it come from? From our five-year-old Brown Swiss cow, Milka.

The milk is treated and the yoghurt is prepared by dairy enthusiasts in our community of two hundred, where it is enjoyed by children and adults alike.

Brown Swiss cows are known for their docile temperament, longevity, good feet and legs, and high production. Originally bred in the Alps, they may be one of the oldest breeds of dairy cows, and the protein-to-fat ratio in their milk is ideal for cheese-making. One Brown Swiss, Glad Ray EJ Paris of Ohio, presently holds the world dairy record for lifetime combined pounds of protein and fat; she is still going strong at age seventeen.

Named after the Swiss milk-chocolate brand, Milka is treated royally by everyone involved in our community barn – from the kindergartners who poke handfuls of hay to her through the fence, to the schoolchildren who help feed, water, and brush her, to the adult volunteers who milk her each morning and evening and then pasteurize the daily yield. Other volunteers include the electrician who fixed the motor on the vacuum pump, the plumber who put a new floor drain in her stall, and the farmer who grinds, mixes, and delivers her feed. It truly takes a whole village to raise a cow.

She accepts all this attention with unassuming aloofness, or with a playful kick and a run around her pasture, her tail slapped up over her back. In return, she presented us last year with a healthy bull calf who now weighs seven hundred pounds, and she gave us 17,833 pounds of milk – more than eleven times her body weight – during her ten-month lactation.

Milka is a teacher, too, if we are wise enough to listen – she shows us how to responsibly care for her and for the rest of God's creation. By her behavior, she lets us know that if we keep her clean, dry, and comfortable, she will do her best to produce milk. A bemused shake of the head gently rebukes anyone who splashes her when filling the water tub. She tells us when she wants to be milked and when her udder is sore. (If it is, there's always a reason, and she makes it clear that we had better fix the problem fast!) She is curious, investigating anything new in her domain; on rainy days my black umbrella is closely eyed and thoroughly sniffed. We too should be attentive to and curious about the world around us.

Milka moderates the behavior of us humans who care for her. If we rush and are impatient, she becomes nervous. When we treat her well, she responds calmly and generously. Perhaps, in reality, it takes a whole cow to raise a village. ⇝

Mahlon Vanderhoof is a teacher at the Fox Hill Bruderhof community in Walden, New York.

Above: Milka, the community cow, poses for her portait, painted by one of her loyal fans.

Egon Schiele, *The Bridge*

Waging Peace in the Culture Wars

R. R. RENO

Toward a Civilization of Love

CHRISTIANITY is a fighting faith. We're called to gird our loins with truth and to put on the breastplate of righteousness, so that we can contend against the principalities and powers that rule in the present darkness (Eph. 6:11–14). And rule they do. We are living in an era of transition. Increasingly self-confident secular Americans, many very powerful, are frustrated with the residual influence of a Bible-formed worldview. They tire of the limitations Judeo-Christian morality puts on personal decisions about sex, family, and marriage. They're indifferent to the soul-destroying effects of pornography. They turn away from the now widespread moral chaos among the poorest and most vulnerable, focusing instead on the things they want: abortion on demand should contraception fail, greater freedom to use an accelerating technology of reproduction should nature not cooperate, and the option of doctor-assisted suicide at the end of life should the trials of suffering and death be too daunting.

All of us feel in our bones that a great deal is at stake, and we can't simply step aside. "Take the whole armor of God, that you may be able to withstand in the evil day, and having done all, to stand" (Eph. 6:13). The truth demands our loyalty. Furthermore, Christ's commandment that we love our neighbor surely means speaking up for the moral order God has inscribed into every heart. We owe our neighbors, Christian or not, a faithful witness to truth, even when those truths are controversial. Even when our witness gets us labeled as "culture warriors." Even when our witness upsets the status quo and enflames political passions. The prophets of Israel did not come to bring peace, but the sword that is the Word of God.

Though we feel the dark undertow of post-Christian culture, Christ calls us to do more than stand against evil, denounce error, and fight against the corruptions and betrayals of moral truth. The armor of God includes a sword, but we're to beat it into a plowshare. "Blessed are the peacemakers, for they shall be called sons of God" (Matt. 5:9). Our Lord arrays us for battle, yes, but he does so with the "equipment of the gospel of peace" (Eph. 6:15). The most profound Christian vocation in the public square is not to win debates and elections, but to build a civilization of love.

This is not easy today. In my view, the rancor that now greets Christian morality presents a significant spiritual challenge. When our witness is part of a society-wide cultural conflict, when once widely accepted moral truths are viewed as partisan political stances, our words can too easily rend the fabric of society. Our witness can heighten conflict rather than contribute to a civilization of love. Thus an important question all of us face: How, for the sake of peace in our society, are we to wield the sharp, sometimes flaming words of truth?

Saint Paul gives us a clear principle: We are to speak the truth in love (Eph. 4:15). Love seeks the higher peace of unity in Christ. In all we say and do, we should aspire to love's heights. However, in civic life we may do better to start with a more modest enterprise, which is to develop good habits of public speech, beginning with the virtue of civility.

The Bible itself can help us become more civil, and in so doing turn our truth-telling, if not into peacemaking, then at least into something that preserves the possibilities of peace in our era of intense cultural conflict. In this regard, the Golden Rule teaches the most obvious lesson: Do unto others as you would have them do unto you (Matt. 7:12).

R. R. Reno is the editor of First Things *magazine and the author of* Fighting the Noonday Devil: And Other Essays Personal and Theological *(Eerdmans, 2011).*

I don't want others to pretend that they agree with me when they don't, and I find it condescending when people remain silent because they think I might be hurt by disagreement. The Golden Rule does not warrant shrinking from sometimes tough and sharply worded encounters. It is not a counsel of niceness, which at best produces an artificial peace in which everyone works very hard to avoid controversial topics. Admittedly, to agree to disagree makes a truce of sorts, and there's a proper place for it in public life – we may need a cooling-off period, as it were.

But the peace of Christ that passes all understanding is not the merely negative peace of an absence of conflict. It's the peace of union with him, and with our brothers and sisters in Christ. Peacemaking involves community building, which can't be done if we refuse to engage each other about the moral underpinnings that shape the civic life we share. That requires us to do unto others as we would have them do unto us: engaging them as adults who can bear disagreement without rancor.

So by all means there should be public debate. The question is, will such conversations be civil, or will they be saturated with ad hominem attacks, as today's debates often are? Here the Golden Rule's lesson for civility is obvious. I don't like having my views distorted, nor do I enjoy it when others suggest that I

Paul Klee, *City of Churches*

have mean, selfish motives; accordingly, I must refrain from treating my opponents in these ways. While it may be true that the thinking of today's secular liberals has been distorted by the modern diminution of moral authority to the sovereign self, it's not true that they are motivated by a selfish interest to make moral truth revolve around themselves. On the contrary, many are motivated by a profound regard for the rights and freedoms of others. The same goes for me, of course. I'm often the "conservative" voice arguing against secular-liberal efforts to change our laws and social norms to reflect "progressive" views. But that does not mean I "fear change" or am in some way psychologically incapable of engaging other views.

One of the most uncivil and destructive aspects of today's progressive project in morality and culture has been to label morally reasoned opposition to same-sex marriage as "homophobia." It is politically convenient to summarily dismiss those who disagree rather than showing how they reason wrongly. But doing so erodes civility. The Golden Rule stipulates that, no matter how deeply we disagree, we must take others seriously as moral agents who seek to promote the common good.

To the Golden Rule we can add another basic moral principle: Saint Paul's exhortation to refrain from doing evil for the sake of some greater or higher good (Rom. 3:8). Political debate is a contact sport. It involves sharply worded polemics, and rightly so, because a great deal is at stake. It's no sin against the Golden Rule to refuse to speak of abortion supporters as "pro-choice," saying instead, "pro-abortion." A picture of an aborted child is shocking, but then the reality is as well. Civility does not shy away from forceful words and images that our adversaries would like to parry, dismiss, and hide.

All the same, we need to be sure to discipline our interventions. We need to set aside the temptation to score merely rhetorical victories that sway the minds of others with falsehoods and half-truths – even when doing so promises us a tactical advantage. Prevarication corrupts the public realm, because it creates an atmosphere of distrust. Though it's less obvious, the same goes for a persistent refusal to acknowledge the implications of one's own positions. When we fight for policies that provide public benefits for illegal immigrants, we're dishonest if we refuse to allow that such policies, however proper from a moral perspective, will encourage more illegal immigration.

T HE GOLDEN RULE and the principle that the ends do not justify the means have an obvious relevance for sustaining civility in public life. But perhaps more important is Jesus' assertion that his kingdom is not of this world (John 18:36).

The passions of our faith should be fiery and urgent. We cannot believe in Christ too much. We cannot be too committed to the community gathered in his name. However, this never-too-much principle does not apply to our judgments about the common good and our roles as neighbors and citizens. Christ's lordship makes a difference in this world, which is why we rightly engage in public debate and seek to fulfill our responsibilities as both Christians and citizens. But it is not of this world. Our deepest convictions are at stake in debates about abortion, war-making, same-sex marriage, and many other controversial topics. But our souls are not. We rightly anguish over the moral destiny of our nation, yet always remember that America is an earthly city, not the heavenly city. Thus, our contributions to public debate should not be overloaded with feelings of final and ultimate urgency.

> How, for the sake of peace in our society, are we to wield sharp, sometimes flaming words of truth?

To know that Christ's kingdom is not of this world should not be interpreted as a reason to be nonpartisan. His teachings had relevance in first-century Jerusalem, where he overturned the tables of the moneychangers, and they have relevance here and now. As we seek to live and speak in accord with Christ's words, we cannot control how the world responds to us. A generation ago, there was nothing partisan about a Christian view of marriage. Neither Democrats nor Republicans resisted no-fault divorce. It was an era of bipartisan negligence. Meanwhile, gay marriage was a non-starter. This has changed. Now marriage is a hot-button issue that political operatives use to agitate their bases. "Marriage equality" becomes a slogan on the left, "family values" on the right.

When biblical morality becomes a political football, we need to follow another of Jesus' teachings: "Be wise as serpents and innocent as doves" (Matt. 10:16). We should be aware of how our convictions are being manipulated in the political process. Still, we cannot let the cynicism of the world silence our witness, which is what happens when we shy away from issues in order to avoid being partisan. If our attempts to do justice to the Bible's vision of the common good lead to us being labeled partisan, then so be it.

We will certainly need to be serpent-wise as we build alliances to achieve political effectiveness. It is not a violation of civility to make shrewd decisions about what to play down and what to play up as we enter into effective coalitions. The fact that the Democratic and Republican Parties are extremely imperfect political vehicles for any Christian vision of the common good does not disqualify them. It would be political pharisaism to refuse to pollute oneself with the realities of public life in a fallen world.

But we can't only be wise as serpents. We also need to cultivate a degree of political innocence that's willing to keep speaking the truth even when the pundits and politicians tell us it's an electoral loser. We should by all means seek to make our Christian witness politically influential; however, we should do so knowing that this world is passing away. If we keep in mind that Christ reigns already, it takes some of the sting out of political debates. We should seek to attain a holy indifference to our political effectiveness. After all, we are debating first things, not final things.

WE EXHIBIT the virtue of civility in many ways. To be civil means showing hospitality, inviting others to join in our common life – even the stranger and sojourner. Civility at its best is capacious. It trusts that those with whom we share civil

society are well intentioned, even when misguided. Civility encourages a spirit of fraternal correction, something we need in an age of denunciation and Twitter mobs that gather to celebrate cyber-lynchings. In these and other ways, civility foreshadows love's vocation of peacemaking. A society is civil because we are united in a partial but real friendship, even as we joust over the direction of our culture.

Multifaceted though it may be, civility is primarily a discipline of the tongue, as the Letter of James makes clear. Faced with a church riven with divisions of wealth, status, and theological opinion (which is to say every church to some degree or another), in the third chapter James turns his attention to the community's leaders and how they speak. Insofar as any of us write for journals and newspapers, or speak at podiums and in the media, we too are being addressed by James. His word of counsel: bridle your tongue, for though a little member, it is capable of guiding the body politic, steering the ship of state – and setting the public square ablaze with rancor, distrust, and ill will.

That James should emphasize the need for leaders to discipline their tongues is not surprising. The sins of the tongue are so troubling that they get double treatment in the Ten Commandments: Do not take the Lord's name in vain. Do not bear false witness. This double emphasis prefigures Jesus' teaching that we should give special attention to what comes out of our mouths. As James points out, with our tongues we both bless God and curse our neighbors. We should seek to do the former, not the latter.

We inevitably speak with anger, derogate others, and speak falsehoods. We are political

> # We should seek to attain a holy indifference to our political effectiveness.

animals with political instincts. Like all of our instincts, the political ones that motivate us to engage in public life – and make us vulnerable to what others say and do in our shared civic culture – can become enflamed and unruly. Our devotion to truth and justice can become disordered, leading us to sin with our tongues, igniting destructive fires in our common life. Against this tendency, James urges us to seek to discipline our tongues so that we can bring in the harvest of righteousness. He who gains command over his tongue, James says in so many words, has in an important sense attained perfection.

We need some of that perfection right now. In the face of intensifying conflict over moral and cultural issues, our society strains to maintain the bonds of civic friendship, the positive peace of fraternal loyalty. What we have to say as Christians is important. Our society needs to hear from us. Yet many of our fellow citizens now see us as dangerous zealots committed to an antiquated, oppressive faith. As we engage them, we need to embody the virtue of civility. If our political passions are properly disciplined and our tongues bridled, then perhaps it will be possible to have fundamental debates of profound moral significance and public consequence – and do so while sustaining the bonds of loyalty and civic friendship that makes an aggregation of individuals into a nation.

This can be done, and our communities of faith have an important role to play. While living in Omaha, Nebraska, I was a member of a church recently formed by the merger of an all-black congregation and an all-white one. There were many conflicts, but we painfully, slowly grew together. At one point, with our interracial challenges in mind, one of the older black members, Richard, a congregational leader, arranged for the church council to view a movie about the Tuskegee airmen. They were the black pilots and crew who, during World War II, suffered discrimination during their training. Their story was painfully ironic given that they were preparing to risk their lives to defend America.

After we watched the film, Richard was the first person to talk. It was evident that he was deeply moved by the film, and with tears in his eyes, he said, "How could we have treated those men so poorly?" I was taken aback. Richard was old enough to have grown up under Jim Crow, but he was saying *we,* not pointing to *me.*

I knew him well enough to recognize that it was patriotism that motivated him to say *we.* Too often progressives downplay this important emotion of loyalty, and Christians often join in, observing that patriotism makes an idol of the state. There are excesses to criticize. But patriotism can also encourage a self-giving to the common good. It is more powerful than civility, which for the most part preserves and protects civic friendship rather than building and promoting it. Building such friendship was exactly what Richard was doing when his patriotism led him to identify with, rather than repudiate or denounce, those who had discriminated against the Tuskegee airmen – and against him and his grandparents, great-grandparents, and great-great-grandparents who were born as slaves. Given the bitter suffering endured by black Americans, it was a remarkable gesture of civic hospitality that exceeded the bounds of civility in the same way love transcends duty. He took the lead, inviting us all to repent together rather than re-litigate and re-fight old struggles. In that moment I had a glimpse of what it means to build a civilization of love. ⇒

Carl Larsson, *Fishing*

INSIGHTS
on Peacemaking

CHARLES SPURGEON

It should ever be remembered that we have no war against persons, and that the weapons which we use are not such as are forged for the deadly conflicts of mankind. The wars of a Christian are against principles, against sins, against the miseries of mankind, against that Evil One who has led man astray from his Maker. Our wars are against the iniquity which keeps man an enemy to himself. The weapons that we use are holy arguments and consecrated lives, devotion and prayer to God, teaching and example. . . . Ours is battling for the peace, and fighting for rest. We disturb the world to make it quiet, and turn it upside down to set it right. . . . We have no sympathy with any other war, but count it an evil of the direst sort, let it be disguised as it may.

Charles Spurgeon (1834–1892) was England's most renowned preacher in the late nineteenth century. At age twenty he became pastor of London's New Park Street Chapel. His sermons reached an estimated ten million people.

JEANNETTE RANKIN

Boundaries are contacts as well as limits. At what point do the interests of our country meet and possibly conflict with those of other countries? What are our real interests anyway and are they worth a war for their protection? And are the interests in question those of the nation as a whole or merely those of a small group of men or even of a single man? Are such clashes anyway settled better by heat and conflict or by a reasonable adjustment?

Jeannette Rankin (1880–1973) was the first woman to be elected to the US Congress. A lifelong pacifist, she voted against US entry into both world wars. Rankin also championed the rights of women, children, and the poor.

ANDRÉ TROCMÉ

Perhaps it is true that certain violent remedies employed against tyrants have put an end to certain forms of evil, but they have not eliminated evil. Evil itself will take root elsewhere, as we have seen through history. The fertilizer that stimulates its growth is yesterday's violence. Even "just wars" and "legitimate defense" bring vengeance in their train. Fresh crimes invariably ensue. But the future of the person who turns to God is not determined by the past, and therefore neither is the future of humanity. God's forgiveness creates the possibility of an entirely new future. The cross breaks the cycle of violence.

Pastor André Trocmé (1901–1971) led a non-violent resistance movement in Le Chambon, France, during World War II. He and fellow villagers provided refuge for an estimated 2,500 Jews. After the war, he served as European secretary for the Fellowship of Reconciliation. ➤

Charles Spurgeon, "A Good Soldier of Jesus Christ" (Sermon No. 938), June 26, 1870 at the Metropolitan Tabernacle, Newington. Jeanette Rankin, "Peace and the Disarmament Conference," in *Two Votes Against War: And Other Writings on Peace* (A.J. Muste Memorial Institute, 2001). André Trocmé, *Jesus and the Nonviolent Revolution* (Plough, 2003) 152.

Photograph by Joel Dinda

Forgive the Unforgivable?

Obeying the Unsoothing Gospel

JOHANN CHRISTOPH ARNOLD

> IT IS NECESSARY, it seems to me, to begin from the fact that, yes, there is the unforgivable. Is this not, in truth, the only thing there is to forgive? The only thing that calls for forgiveness? If one is only prepared to forgive what appears forgivable, what the church calls "venial sin," then the very idea of forgiveness would disappear. . . . There is only forgiveness, if there is any, where there is the unforgivable.
>
> *Jacques Derrida, "On Forgiveness"*

Human nature being what it is, the ability to see a brother or sister in every person we meet is a grace. Even our relationships with those who are closest to us are clouded now and then, if only by petty grievances. True peace with others requires effort. Sometimes it demands the readiness to yield; at other times, the willingness to be frank. Today we may need humility to remain silent; tomorrow, courage to confront or speak out. One thing remains constant, however: if we seek peace in our relationships, we must be willing to forgive over and over.

Forgiving has nothing to do with being fair, or with excusing wrongdoing; in fact, it may mean pardoning someone for something inexcusable. When we excuse someone, we brush his mistake aside. When we forgive someone, there may be good reason to hold onto our hurt, but we let go of it anyway. We refuse to seek revenge. Our forgiveness may not always be accepted, yet the act of reaching out our hand in reconciliation saves us from anger

. . . continued on page 21

Johann Christoph Arnold, a regular Plough *contributor, is the author of* Seeking Peace: Notes and Conversations along the Way *(Plough, 2014), from which this article is taken. For Bill Pelke's story and other accounts of forgiveness, visit* www.journeyofhope.org.

"Peace Be Unto You!"

JOHN STOTT

I**T IS THE EVENING** of the first Easter Day. For fear of the Jewish leaders, the disciples have met secretly, behind closed doors. Through these closed doors comes the risen Jesus and stands in their midst. He has already appeared privately to Mary Magdalene and Peter, to the other women, and the two Emmaus disciples. This, however, is the first official appearance to the Twelve.

His commission to them is in striking contrast to their actual situation. They are terrified, but he tells them to have no fear and rather to be of good courage. They are in hiding, but he bids them throw open the closed doors and, risking the dangers of persecution and death, to march out to the spiritual conquest of the world.

On this occasion, he spoke four short sentences – of greeting, of command, and of promise. "Peace be unto you. . . ."

The church's very first need, before it can begin to engage in evangelism, is an experience and an assurance of Christ's peace – peace of conscience through his death that banishes sin, peace of mind through his resurrection that banishes doubt. Jesus repeated his greeting for emphasis. "Peace be unto you," he said, "peace be unto you."

It is utterly impossible to preach the gospel of peace to others unless we ourselves have peace. Indeed, the greatest single reason for the church's evangelistic disobedience centers in the church's doubts. We are not sure if our own sins are forgiven. We are not sure if the gospel is true. And so, because we doubt, we are dumb. We need to hear again Christ's word of peace, and see again his hands and his side. Once we are glad that we have seen the Lord, and once we have clearly recognized him as our crucified and risen savior, then nothing and no one will be able to silence us. ⬦

From "The Great Commission" by John Stott, published in *One Race, One Gospel, One Task,* Volume 1, edited by Carl F. H. Henry and W. Stanley Mooneyham, World Wide Publications, 1967. © 1967 John R.W. Stott. Courtesy of the John Stott Literary Executors.

Continued from page 19

and indignation. Even if we remain wounded, a forgiving attitude will prevent us from lashing back at someone who has caused us pain. And it can strengthen our resolve to forgive again the next time we are hurt. Dorothy Day writes:

> God is on the side even of the unworthy, as we know from the story Jesus told of the prodigal son. . . . Readers may claim that the prodigal son returned penitent to his father's house. But who knows, he might have gone out and squandered money on the next Saturday night, he might have refused to help with the farm work and asked to be sent to finish his education instead, thereby further incurring his brother's righteous wrath. . . . Jesus has another answer to that one: to forgive one's brother seventy times seven. There are always answers, although they are not always calculated to soothe.

Bill Pelke

Strangely, those who suffer the worst things in life often forgive most readily. Bill Pelke, a Vietnam veteran from Indiana whom I met at an anti–death penalty event, lost his grandmother to a brutal murder, yet found closure in seeking reconciliation with the teenager who killed her.

Bill's grandmother was an outgoing woman who gave Bible lessons to children in her neighborhood. One afternoon in May 1985 she opened the door to four girls from the local high school several blocks away. Before she knew it, her attackers had knocked her to the floor. Minutes later, the house ransacked, they fled the premises in her old car, leaving her on the floor, bleeding to death from multiple stab wounds. Bill remembers:

> The girls were caught giving joy rides to friends in the stolen car. Later they went to trial. Sentencing came fifteen months later: one girl got thirty-five years, two got sixty years, and

the last, Paula Cooper, got death. I was satisfied that at least one of them would be executed: I felt that if they weren't, the court would be saying my grandmother wasn't important, and I felt that she was a very important person.

> About four months after Paula was sentenced, I broke up with a girl I had been dating. I was trying to get the relationship back together and was very depressed. I couldn't find peace about anything.

> Then one day at work, while operating an overhead crane (I worked for Bethlehem Steel), I was thinking about why things hadn't worked out, also with my grandmother, and I just started praying. "Why, God? Why?" Suddenly I thought about Paula – this young girl, the youngest female in the country on death row – and I pictured her saying, "What have I done? What have I done?" I remembered the day Paula was sentenced to death; I recalled her grandfather in court, wailing, "They're killing my baby." He was escorted from the room. There were tears rolling down his cheeks. . . .

> I began to think of my grandmother, her faith, and what the Bible has to say about forgiveness. I recalled three verses: the one which says that for God to forgive you, you first need to forgive others; the one where Jesus tells Peter to forgive "seventy times seven"; the one where Jesus says, when he is being crucified, "Father, forgive them, for they don't know what they are doing." Paula didn't know what she was doing. When a girl stabs a woman thirty-three times, she is not in her right mind.

> Suddenly I felt I had to forgive her. I prayed, right there and then, that God would give me love and compassion for her. That prayer changed my life. I no longer wanted her to die in the electric chair. What would an execution solve for me or anyone else?

Bill added, "When I had gone to the crane I was a defeated person: forty-five minutes later I emerged a completely different man."

Bill visited Paula several times after her trial and sought to pass on his grandmother's faith to her – not by preaching, but simply by showing her compassion. He is no longer haunted by the image of his beloved grandmother lying butchered on the dining room floor – a room where the family had gathered for many of its happiest occasions. Naturally he still feels pain, yet this pain is mixed with a determination to make sure that other people are spared the agony of bitterness that he had to work through. "As long as I kept hating those girls, they continued to control my life. Once I chose to forgive them, I became free."

A committed activist in the growing restorative justice movement, Bill spent years travelling up and down the country with an organization called "Journey of Hope: from Violence to Healing." He is also a member of Murder Victims' Families for Reconciliation. "Forgiveness," he says, "is the only route from violence to healing. It spares you the corrosion of hatred and gives you freedom again to be at peace inside your own skin." (In June 2013, thanks in part to Bill's efforts, Paula was released from prison after serving twenty-seven years.)

Most of us do not have to deal directly with murder; and many of the things we obsess over are even laughable by comparison. Still we may have a hard time forgiving. Especially if our resentment has grown over a long period, it will take time and effort to root out. And whether the hurt is real or imagined, it will eat away at us as long as we nurse it.

Not that we should swallow our hurts. On the contrary, people who push their grievances down into their subconscious in an attempt to forget them only cripple themselves. Before we can forgive a hurt, we must be able to name it. Sometimes it may not be possible (or helpful, even if it is possible) to confront the person we are struggling to forgive, and then the best solution is to share our pain with someone else we trust. Once we have done this, we must let go. Otherwise we may remain resentful forever, waiting for an apology that never comes. And we will remain separated from God.

> As long as we hold a grudge against someone, the door to God will be closed. It will be absolutely closed, with no way to him. I am sure that many prayers are not heard because the person praying has a grudge against someone, even if he or she is not aware of it. If we want God's peace in our hearts, we must first learn to forgive. (J. Heinrich Arnold, *Discipleship*)

Naturally we must seek to be forgiven too. After all, each of us is a sinner in God's eyes, even if our "goodness" prevents us from seeing ourselves in that light. A legend about Brother Angelo, a monk in Francis of Assisi's order, illustrates the problem beautifully.

On Christmas Eve, Brother Angelo cleans his simple mountain hut and decorates it for Mass. He says his prayers, sweeps the hearth, hangs a kettle over the fire, and then sits back to wait for Brother Francis, whom he expects later in the day. Just then three outlaws appear at the door, begging for food. Frightened and angry, Brother Angelo sends them away empty-handed, scolding and warning them that thieves are damned to hellfire.

When Francis arrives, he senses that something is not right. Brother Angelo then tells him about his visitors, and Francis sends him up into the mountains with a jug of wine and a loaf, to find them and ask their forgiveness. Brother Angelo is indignant. Unlike Francis, he cannot see the wild men as brothers – only as outlaws. He sets out obediently, however, and by nightfall (having followed the men's footsteps in the snow) he finds them and makes amends. Some time later, the legend goes, they leave their cave and join the order. ⤳

Errand

The fawn was
born beneath the hydrangea I had mistaken,
        for a year, as a young oak.

I squatted there. No
fear. It lay alone
        in the leaves, and at my near touch a tuft

of its skin (you couldn't
call it
        hide, barely fur, still birth-

smeared in smatters
of pale gray spots) –
        one tuft of skin quivered, as

though cold.
Even this first day
        the doe had gone to find herself

something to eat
in a better yard. Error on
        error, a life amasses.

Do you believe
the old poet – not
        to be born is reckoned best

of all?
So let's ask
        the bird dog gagging at his chain

two yards over, bloody with boredom.
Ask the night-
        black vultures, kettling

over the neighbor's burn pile.
I had somewhere
        to go. I don't know where, but

how could it
matter, so much, to go?
        Smell of snow an hour

before it falls,
then doesn't. Soft leather
        nose of the fawn, wet in my palm

where it nestled its warm
jaw in. To make
        a cathedral (I should have stayed) of such things . . .

DAVID BAKER

أحلامنا

CAT CARTER

The Children of War

and the Dreams They Dream

"Why are you asking me about access to food and water in my country when I have seen my friends executed in front of me? Why don't you ask about that?"

Hassan, age fourteen

Hassan, age fourteen, lives with his parents and brothers in a single tent in the Za'atari camp in Jordan. Sixty-five percent of the camp residents are children.

Fourteen-year-old Hassan's question caught me off-guard. It was early in Syria's civil war, and I was talking with refugee children on the Syria-Lebanon border, hoping to discern their needs. I thought I knew what I'd hear about: long bread queues, dirty drinking water, fear of shells landing on your home perhaps, the occasional story of loss. . . . But nothing prepared me for what I heard. In the maelstrom of war, violence is meted out by adults – but children get hurt.

International law bans recruitment of children in armed conflict. Yet worldwide, up to 300,000 children are used. Some are forced to fight, lay mines, or carry weapons. Others become spies or messengers. Children may be captured and imprisoned if suspected – or if parents are thought likely to pay for their release.

Those not directly involved suffer too, because the health infrastructure is an early casualty in any war. Hospitals tend to focus on

---

Over the last seven years, Cat Carter's work with Save the Children, the international relief organization, has taken her to Haiti, Indonesia, Kenya, Ethiopia, and the Philippines. Recently she has been recording the stories of children in Syria, South Sudan, Gaza, and eastern Ukraine. She lives and blogs in London. www.savethechildren.org

getting fighters back to the frontline; mothers and children take lower priority. Even where this is not the case, when healthcare facilities are destroyed or short-staffed and supplies have run out, it is extremely difficult for doctors and nurses to give adequate care. In Syria, an estimated 60 percent of hospitals have been damaged or destroyed, and nearly half the doctors have fled. In 2014 in Aleppo, the country's largest city, only thirty-six doctors remained of the 2,500 who'd been there before the conflict began.

Even preventable illnesses kill in warzones. If standing in line for immunization means risking being bombed, or if travelling across town means becoming a sniper target, families understandably stay home. The consequence is an unvaccinated generation. Epidemics are spawned in the crowded, dirty conditions that war creates; and where children are exhausted and weakened by stress and hunger, they become further vulnerable. Up to 30 percent of children who contract measles during humanitarian emergencies are likely to die.

Schools, like hospitals, are protected under international law, yet in recent conflicts, schools have been deliberately targeted. Warring groups have discovered that aiming a tank at a school is exceptionally effective – few villagers will continue any protest in face of so dire a threat. And if a school is turned into a place to store weapons or fire missiles from, the adverse impact is double: the building cannot be used for education, and it loses civilian status under international law.

On behalf of Save the Children, I've stayed in a number of war-torn countries as well as in refugee camps on their borders. My role is to listen to teenagers and children, and to record what they tell me. I sometimes wish I could dismiss their accounts as wild imaginings. I can't. I've seen torture scars on nine-year-olds and bullet wounds on ten-year-olds. I've listened to youngsters describe how it feels to be part of a human shield or to collect their siblings' body parts from the street. Mothers have shown me photos of their dead children. I've watched proud men weep.

I don't think I'll ever be able to forget what I have seen and heard. That is as it should be. I don't want to forget.

I relate several instances here. I've changed the individuals' names, because it took great courage for each to share his or her experiences with me, and I do not want any to be harmed as a result.

Giving these children a voice is what drives me. Even if their stories are not widely heard, I have an obligation to pass them on. At least these children's accounts are now on record. They are part of history.

Fadi is ten when I speak with him in a camp outside Syria; he was nine when his village came under siege. With his father away, Fadi became man of the house. His mother tells me he insisted on fetching the family's food and water, even when bullets were flying. He shrugs. "Some children get afraid and hide or cry. Others are like me." He is nonchalant, but I sense that he is pleased to have his courage acknowledged.

Although Fadi did his best, supplies ran out. With no safe routes in or out of the village, families were trapped between armed men and hunger. "People kept trying to leave in groups of maybe ten or twenty. Larger groups would be killed. There was a crossing we called the 'death journey.' It was potluck whether or not you would be shot going through. You might

> "Some children get afraid and hide or cry. Others are like me."
>
> *Fadi, age ten*

Fadi, age ten, plays war games with his friends at the home in the Lebanese town where he and his family arrived a month before.

get across – or you might not. It was so difficult and dangerous; our hearts were racing until we got here."

I ask Fadi what his village was like before he left. "I have seen many bodies – in the streets, thrown outside homes, even in the river. When they see a child, they shoot without hesitating. Some people you just never find.

"They aimed missiles toward our school. When the missiles hit, they destroyed half the building. I was not at school that day, but I saw it burning."

Fadi says he wants to talk about these things, and words pour from him. But then he adds that he is certain I will never understand. "Honestly, if I told you what Syria was like, and what those men have done to us, you would not believe me."

When I meet Nada in Gaza during the 2014 conflict there, she is five years old. But she has lost her ability to speak, and nightmares prevent sleep. She cries almost constantly.

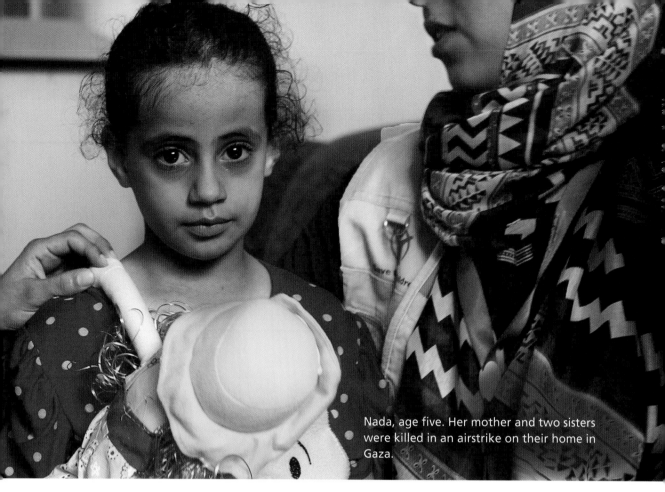

Nada, age five. Her mother and two sisters were killed in an airstrike on their home in Gaza.

Nada's father, Ahmad, takes me down the shrapnel-strewn steps of their home, gesturing at a blue bicycle under the stairs. I'm perplexed – it's just an old bike . . . Ahmad speaks in rapid Arabic. When bombs started falling two weeks ago, he hurried his pregnant wife and two of his five daughters under these stairs to be safe from falling debris, moving the bike out of the way. Then he rushed upstairs for his other three daughters.

Pausing a long moment, Ahmad points at the door behind me. I turn and see shrapnel holes big as dinner plates. I turn slowly back, realization dawning: There are matching holes behind the bicycle; the same shrapnel had torn through his wife and daughters.

Ahmad can't forgive himself for hiding them here. The bike was unharmed.

The two girls, age three and thirteen, died immediately; their mother took longer. Ahmad has only just finished cleaning up under the stairs. He's put the bike back, because – he shrugs sadly – he doesn't know what else to do with it.

Of his surviving daughters, two remain in the hospital with severe injuries, while Nada is physically unhurt but emotionally broken.

Ahmad asks my advice. What can he say to Nada to make things right again for her?

Eleven-year-old Omar argued with his cousin Fatima. She was nine, and the two of them had been playing together at Omar's home that morning. Fatima ran home, upset by their quarrel. Soon after she arrived back home, a shell hit her house. It killed the entire family.

Omar believed Fatima's death was his fault. If they hadn't argued . . . If he hadn't upset her . . . If, if, if . . .

Omar, age eleven, lives with his family in the Za'atari refugee camp, Jordan. "I was so scared my tongue was frozen, I couldn't even talk."

Omar is not the only child carrying this kind of weight; too many think they are somehow to blame for the tragedies around them. For a whole year, Omar was unable to speak of his torment. Only after numerous conversations with Save the Children's team, and group sessions with other children, did he start to shake his feeling that he was to blame for Fatima's death.

Even now I can give little detail because he finds it so difficult to discuss his story – and I do not want to make it harder for him, so I do not press.

In a camp for Syrian refugees in Lebanon, a mother, Jemilah recounts, "We were hiding in our basement. It was dark because the electricity had been cut. With no phone, we knew nothing of the outside world. No one could bring supplies into our village, and no one could escape either. In those four days

underground, my fourteen-year-old son ate only half a piece of bread and drank two glasses of water. Then everything ran out.

"We had a baby with us, my granddaughter Safaa. She was one year old, so my daughter wanted to wean her, but she would cry loudly. We had seen before that a crying baby attracts the attention of armed men; they come to find the baby, and kill the whole family. Every time she cried, my daughter breastfed her, so she would not get us all killed.

"My son said to me, 'I am a man, I am not afraid.' But when another family arrived and reported that men were searching basements for families, my son became terrified. He started crying on my shoulder, asking what would happen if we were found. I knew the answer. But I lied. I said I would save him, that everything would be OK.

"Every day more families joined us when their homes were destroyed. It was a large basement – almost a whole floor of the house. By the end there were over a hundred people, still with no food or water. It was desperate. When we realized armed men were approaching street by street, we decided to flee. Not all of us, but many. Our destiny was death if we stayed. We decided not to wait for death to come for us.

"We went out to the street. It was six o'clock in the morning, a new day. We ran to our car. It was a small car, only two doors, and all the children crammed in. There were eight people in the car. My husband, who drove, was the only man. The rest were mothers and small children.

> ## "Tell me that you will tell everyone what you have heard here today."
>
> *Jemilah, a mother*

"We turned down a side road to avoid snipers, but what we saw was horror. Whole families that we knew, who had lived in our street and played with our children, were stood against the wall and shot. They were being executed, even the children. We screamed and turned another way. We were shot at, but my husband knew the area and we managed to escape by going down a small track between farms. I don't know what happened to the other families in the basement.

"There are still many families inside the town. They cannot move; they cannot leave. There is nothing for them. Shops are looted and supplies cannot get in. There is no medicine, no food, no clean water. They cannot get to the farms to take fruit or potatoes. So those families are already dead.

"When I think of Syria, all I can see is this – and the mountains of bodies. The night before we fled there was a mass killing; as we were fleeing, we saw bodies, piled up. We saw men using those digger machines to move the bodies because there were too many to bury properly.

"I wish these men doing the killing were from another country, an enemy country. Not this. Not our own people doing this to each other. It's too much to cope with.

"I am telling you this because these men think there will be no evidence of these massacres. They think the bodies will be destroyed and their crimes will never be known.

"Tell me that you will tell everyone what you have heard here today."

One young woman, Roha, is too nervous to let me record the interview or name her country. She is twenty-three, soft-spoken but determined. We sit to discuss the conflict's impact on her family, but the conversation quickly becomes darker.

Roha fled an area in the Middle East known for its heavy fighting. When I assume that was her reason for flight, she shakes her head, and her eyes dart to the men in the room. She asks that they leave, and I feel a creeping sense of foreboding. I've had conversations – too many – which demand that men leave the room, and I know what it means.

"Although the fighting was very bad, we could live with it, we could survive. What we could not live with was the constant threat of rape . . ." Roha trails off. I wait.

Roha says the sexual violence escalated swiftly in her village. One day she emerged after a bout of heavy fighting to find the naked bodies of five girls, all between ten and twelve years old, laid out on the ground – a warning to the community to make no more trouble. It was clear, Roha says, that they had all been sexually assaulted. I don't ask how she knew. I don't want to know.

The stories keep coming – one leads to another, and another, and another – a torrent,

Muna, age five, and Tamer, age three, escaped from Syria into Lebanon with their mother Laila after armed gangs in Syria threatened to kill the family. They hope they will find their father, who fled Syria the previous year to avoid being forced to fight. "We used to live in a small village on the mountain," Laila said. "We owned a big farm, greenhouses, tractors, and a harvester." She and her children now live in an abandoned cowshed.

unstoppable and harrowing. Finally she tells me that she witnessed the sexual assault of a twelve-year-old neighbor through her window. Too terrified to intervene, Roha couldn't move. She is still deeply ashamed that she didn't. The act had been a punishment for the girl's father. As the armed men left, they killed him too.

Once she was sure the men were gone, Roha rushed to help the girl. "She survived. But actually they both died that day, in different ways," Roha says quietly. "I saw this with my own eyes. I can never stop seeing it now."

By now she is in tears. I sit beside her, holding her hand. What else can I do?

Roha composes herself. Suddenly she erupts in anger: at those men for what they did, at herself for what she didn't do. And at her community for refusing to talk about it, for burying such incidents through a sense of shame.

"This is the big issue – but no one will talk about it. Why? Why! Because we are ashamed? Let us instead shame those who do this!" She strikes her hand on the concrete floor, bracelets jangling.

The men re-enter. Abruptly, Roha stands, brushing away tears. She looks at me for a long minute. "Would you like some tea?" she asks.

Wael, a Syrian lad in a Lebanese camp tells me, "I was arrested with hundreds of others. They separated the children. At sixteen, I was the oldest. I can't tell you how many we were, but there were many. We were forced together into a cell. There was nowhere to go – there wasn't even a toilet, just a hole in the floor. If they overheard us talking, we were beaten. So we didn't talk. All we heard was screaming, crying, and then silence.

"There were thirteen or fourteen children whose parents were 'wanted'. They weren't allowed food or water. When it was time to eat, their group was surrounded by armed men who prevented anyone from giving them food. These children were too weak to cry; they just lay on the floor. They were repeatedly beaten with sticks, worse than the rest of us.

"I knew a boy who was part of that group, Ala'a, only six years old. He didn't understand what was happening. His father was part of a rival armed group and was told his child would die unless he gave himself up. He didn't give himself up. Ala'a was tortured more than anyone else in that room. He only survived three days, and then he simply died. I watched him die on the floor. They treated his body like he was a dog.

"By then, I wasn't able to think about anything. I thought I would die in that cell, and I couldn't see past that. When I left that place, I felt I'd escaped death.

"Now, I feel that no one cares about Syria. No one is helping us, and we're dying. If there was even one percent of humanity in the world, this wouldn't happen. I feel like I'm dying from the inside. At least when I die this will be over."

Wael weeps.

"Torture is not only physical, it's mental. When you see women and children scream and die, it has an effect. Every Syrian has been devastated by this war. There's no way I can cope, no way I can turn over a new page. I have seen children slaughtered. I don't think I'll ever be OK again . . . "

Wael doesn't know what happened to the other children.

When his release was eventually secured by his parents, who paid a steep fee, Wael was adamant that he wanted to return to Syria, to fight. But he has changed his mind – he says he has seen too much death and destruction.

Wael now dreams of going back into Syria to encourage and inspire other children, to bring them aid, to urge them not to lose hope – and to work, somehow, for peace.

To tell these stories is not enough, I know. What response could ever be adequate? When families share their experiences with me, I feel honored by their confidence and moved by their courage – yet each time it is also an exquisite pain. Returning from a deployment, I often have nightmares.

On my first day on the job, my boss, Gareth Owen, gave me some advice: Let this work change you. And that is the only conclusion I can offer here. Let these stories change us. Nothing less will do. ⤳

Organizations that help children in war zones urgently need our support. They include:
www.savethechildren.org
www.worldvision.org
www.doctorswithoutborders.org

> Wael now dreams of going back into Syria – to work, somehow, for peace.

Mikalojus Konstantinas Čiurlionis, *The Hymn*, 1904–1905

During his brief creative career, the Lithuanian artist and composer Mikalojus Konstantinas Čiurlionis (1875–1911) produced around four hundred paintings and an equal number of musical works. Čiurlionis stands as a unique figure in European art history. His distinctive talent makes him difficult to classify into any one school; some have called him a symbolist, while others point to his role as a pioneer of abstract art.

Čiurlionis's biography includes striking parallels to the life of Vincent van Gogh. Both artists were driven by an intense search for the transcendent, and both threw themselves with abandon into the quest to express truths that they felt stemmed from a source beyond them. Both collapsed physically and mentally under the immense demands of this creative effort, and both died in their mid-thirties.

Čiurlionis began as a musician, attending the conservatories in Warsaw and Leipzig. Despite his achievements as a composer – his works for orchestra, piano, and string quartet are still performed – he developed a growing passion for expressing his visions through painting.

In the artworks he produced during the final three years of his life, he sought to portray the underlying and invisible reality of the world rather than merely its surface. Frequent themes include the beauty of the thoughts of the Creator as well as the struggle of two opposing forces in the spiritual realm. Romain Rolland, the French writer and Nobel laureate, sums it up: "There is a continent for the spirit, and Čiurlionis is its Christopher Columbus." ➤

Vilija Kačergytė-Compy

Vilija Kačergytė-Compy, who grew up admiring Čiurlionis's art in her native Lithuania, is a member of the Bruderhof community in Elka Park, New York. To view more of the artist's work, see www.ciurlionis.eu.

Ben Shahn, *Beatitude*

What Gandhi Taught Me about Jesus

A PASTOR'S MEMOIR

A. C. OOMMEN

FIRST SAW MAHATMA GANDHI when I was twelve, when he came to our state of Kerala in south India to help remove the age-old injustice of caste discrimination. He addressed a huge gathering on a river bed near my school, and I found a seat on the sand near where he was sitting cross-legged on a raised platform. He spoke about vegetarianism, not about national issues, but it impressed me immensely – he spoke in Hindi rather than English, and I saw him as a symbol of the resurgent India.

At that time, Gandhi was already famous in Kerala because of his 1924 action in the nearby town of Vaikom to open the Shiva temple to Hindus of all castes. For centuries, outcastes had been forbidden to enter the temple, and notices even prohibited them from using the town's roads. Gandhi's nonviolent campaign to abolish this humiliating segregation had been the first major test of his teaching of satyagraha ("soul force" or "truth force").

On coming home from hearing Gandhi, I told my mother that I was now a vegetarian. (I

A. C. Oommen, a theologian and pastor in the Church of South India, lives in Kaviyoor, Pathanamthitta District in Kerala, India.

would remain one for the next eighteen years, until moving to Uganda, when I gave it up in order to dine in fellowship with my African brethren.) From that day on, I began to follow Gandhi's teachings. Despite my conflicting feelings toward British missionaries, whom I admired for their sacrificial work to uplift the so-called untouchables in Kerala, I began to participate in the Quit India movement pressing for India's independence from Britain.

Although as a twelve-year-old I would not have been able to articulate what drew me to Gandhi, I now see four facets of his life and teaching as keys to understanding him.

First, truth and nonviolence were identical to him; they supported each other and gave coherence to his life. Nonviolence was not just a methodology or a "Gandhian tactic" as some have labeled it, but his religion itself. Truth is the ultimate reality, the climax of our search – the point where all our coverings and curtains are taken off. We do not know if he saw truth as an idea or as a person ("I am the Truth"), but he openly lived out the answer to the question "What is truth?"

Second, simplicity. Simplicity is the heart of India's age-old spiritual search. To Gandhi it was not just in lifestyle, but simplicity in all his actions. He simplified his dress code from that of the Western lawyer to that of the Indian sadhu, prompting Winston Churchill to call him a "half-naked fakir." Gandhi dressed this way in England as well, even when he met King George V in Buckingham Palace at the king's request. When the British press questioned the appropriateness of this dress for such a meeting, he replied that the king, as emperor of India, was wearing enough for two people, including clothing stolen from India's poor. Gandhi's own simplicity was thus a reflection of his nonviolence and compassion: he felt that if he used anything more than was absolutely necessary, he would be robbing a poorer brother or sister. For the same reason, he always travelled in what some now call the "cattle class" in Indian trains and followed the communal ashram style of living, remaining accessible to all who wished to meet him.

> Gandhi reminded me of Saint John in his old age, who constantly repeated: "Little children, love one another."

Third, Gandhi proclaimed and practiced the dignity of manual labor. He believed that no one has a right to eat unless he is willing to get mud on his hands and participate in the production of food. He taught his students never to make anyone else do a task that we felt to be below our own dignity. Despite being so well known and honored, he cleaned the latrines himself.

Finally, Gandhi's life was transparent. He revealed his mind in advance to all who wanted to catch him for some fault. The secret police officer appointed to watch him for political reasons found him an easy assignment: he just had to ask Gandhi what he was going to speak about, and he would tell him. Yet those of us who admired his profound thoughts and practical actions felt the depth of his vision, his gift of withdrawal in the hurly-burly of an active and busy life, and his ability to relax, reflect, and meditate inside the storm.

I never forgot my boyhood encounter with Gandhi, and his voice continued to influence my life. In 1947, when India became independent,

I was a university student at Calcutta. As the midnight bell rang on August 15, people all over India and beyond listened to the historic speech that Pandit Nehru, our first prime minister and a great disciple of Gandhi, gave at Parliament House in Delhi. But Gandhi was not part of the celebration; with urgent work to do, he had disappeared from the scene.

The reason for his absence was that, as a precondition for India's independence, the country was to be split in two as India and Pakistan. Gandhi had given his consent to this division reluctantly. This was one of the rare occasions when he gave in to others against his inner conviction, which came from a part of his life hidden from others: meditation, silence, and careful listening to the still, small voice within him. One day of each week was strictly observed as a silence day. When he faced important decisions that affected his country, he asked for time to listen to that inner voice. Popular opinion was secondary to his decision-making because history is a dialogue between God and people. The world is pulled from above to a definite destiny, not pushed from behind by a blind force.

Upon partition, India witnessed violence on a scale it had never seen before, especially in Bengal in the east and Punjab in the west; Calcutta was the worst affected city on the eastern front. Thousands of families on both sides of the new line were uprooted. As law and order broke down completely, it was impossible to control the crowds; I saw dead bodies piled up on the roadside. The police and army acknowledged their inability to control the violence.

Then we heard that Gandhi was coming to Calcutta. He had no military protection, and anyone could easily have killed him.

Where are the Christians that live according to the Bible?

He left Delhi unnoticed, traveling by train in a third-class compartment. Arriving in Calcutta's Howrah station, he walked with his stick across the platform and asked for a small tent to be put up in the nearby maidan, where he seated himself on a raised platform. Remarking, "It's better to die than to live in a world of violence," he held a fast unto death.

The first two or three days went by without much change in the communal violence. By the third day, Gandhi was very weak and could not sit up. The news that he was dying spread far and wide. Leaders of the warring Hindus and Muslims came together in an attempt to save his life, promising Gandhi they would lay down their own lives to prevent any more deaths. But Gandhi insisted that he would continue his fast until he saw a real change among the people. It was Gandhi's Satyagraha in action: the innocent taking on the burden of others' sins, and offering his own life as atonement.

Then a miracle took place of which I am an eyewitness. It seemed as if a breath of the Holy Spirit blew across the city. People came out of hiding. They put down their weapons before him, fell prostrate, and asked for his forgiveness. I saw separate processions of the warring Muslim and Hindu communities coming from two sides. Before, they would have attacked each other and none would have been left alive. Now they embraced each other, saying, "We are brothers."

The transformation was deep and the cost of forgiveness great. At that time a Hindu asked Gandhi, "What shall I do? My only son was killed by a Muslim." Straight came the reply: "Forgive. Adopt a Muslim child as your own. His parents may have been killed by Hindus."

And so what the whole police force and the army failed to achieve in Calcutta, Gandhi accomplished in a few days. Lord Mountbatten, former governor general of India, called him India's "one-man army." Gandhi showed that innocent suffering is the most powerful tool to bring peace to a world weary of conflict and war, just as Isaiah wrote in the songs of the suffering servant: "With his stripes we are healed." After establishing peace in Calcutta, Gandhi walked through the villages, and wherever he went the miracle occurred and people abandoned violence. I witnessed this.

Meanwhile, the violence in the northwestern border state of Punjab was even worse than in Calcutta. Gandhi was pained by the daily reports of suffering caused by large scale exodus and violence in the divided region. Through his newspaper, *The Harijan,* he sent out an appeal for volunteers to staff the growing refugee camps. One line struck me at the time: "Where are the Christians that live according to the Bible?" He argued that the Christians, as a minority in India, were not a threat to either the Muslims or the Hindus, and that they could bring the Christian message of reconciliation to both camps.

Having seen the carnage in Bengal, I was deeply moved by Gandhi's call to Christians and found it impossible to study theology under these conditions. I shared my pain with like-minded classmates and we approached the principal of our college for a leave of absence to serve under Gandhi. He tried to dissuade us, arguing that India's churches needed us to study for the future, but finally he gave permission. The National Council of Churches of India agreed to sponsor us. We went back home to Kerala to gather a few other young men who

Ben Shahn, *Gandhi*

wanted to join us, and to bid farewell to our parents and dear ones. None of us were confident we would return home alive.

On our way to the Punjab, we stayed a few days in Delhi, where I met Horace Alexander. He had mediated between Gandhi and Muhammad Ali Jinnah, former leader of the All-India Muslim League and now founder of Pakistan, in a last-minute attempt to avoid partition. Alexander took me to attend the daily prayer meetings at Birla House where Gandhi lived. Exactly at five each afternoon, Gandhi would walk into the maidan supported by a friend and take his seat on a raised platform. We would sing a hymn, often Isaac Watts's "When I Survey the Wondrous Cross." Gandhi especially loved the final verse:

Were the whole realm of nature mine,
That were a present far too small;
Love so amazing, so divine,
Demands my soul, my life, my all.

A passage from the Quran, the Bhagavad Gita, or the Bible would be read. Then Gandhi would speak briefly, followed by a short silence. One day as I sat at his feet, a very agitated Hindu pleaded with Gandhi for permission to retaliate, saying that his whole family had been wiped out by Muslims. Gandhi replied, as he always did: "Forgive. Peace. Love."

It was not easy or cheap for Gandhi to speak of forgiveness. His shoulders would come down as if he was carrying all of India's pain and suffering. He reminded me of Saint John in his old age, who constantly repeated, "Little children, love one another."

At Gandhi's direction, we moved to the refugee camps to get to work. Our first assignment was the Muslim camp in Ambala. On the way, we witnessed the exodus of refugees, walking in lines nearly a mile long. The camp itself was shocking: two hundred thousand people on just over two acres of land. Smallpox and cholera broke out; we hardly had enough time to bury the dead. Then the wounded arrived from trains that had been deliberately derailed. Our main duty was to help the sick and wounded get into the overcrowded trains going to Pakistan.

Next we were assigned to a Hindu camp in Kurukshetra to receive those who were coming in from Pakistan. It was another scene of misery. Each refugee had a bitter story to tell of murder, rape, or fights, and their only thought was revenge. Anything we said about forgiveness, love, or reconciliation meant nothing; they had suffered more than we could imagine. Night after night we returned to our tent and poured out our pain to the Lord.

The great change happened on January 30, 1948. From a broken radio we heard the news that Gandhi had been assassinated – gunned down on his way to the daily prayer meeting, at the same spot where a few months before I had sat at his feet. We returned to the camp, and found it silent for the first time. I saw tears in many eyes that until then had been filled only with lust for revenge. The words spoken in unison were: "He died for our sake."

We packed our things and left to attend the funeral in Delhi. It seemed like a different city. Not a single fire was lit in any of the homes. Broken-hearted crowds pressed toward the van carrying the dead body to the funeral ground. Even people who had been hiding in fear for their lives came out boldly into the streets to catch a glimpse of the dead martyr they adored. We took our stand by the side of the road to witness the procession, with the country's leaders at the front. There was no need for the police or army to keep order. People threw weapons away and joined together, irrespective of caste and religion, to pay homage to the departed leader. I, too, shed tears – not only because of Gandhi, but because his death reminded me of an innocent death two thousand years ago, a death through which abundant life, a life of love and forgiveness, was offered to me.

Thanks to Gandhi's witness, I found my life calling in the ministry of reconciliation. I have worked on race relations in Uganda, on bridging divides in a caste-ridden church in Kerala, and on achieving reconciliation between staff and management as chaplain in a hospital in Vellore. In all this, I have been guided by the life and death of Jesus – the Jesus whom I learned to love more deeply through the life and death of Mahatma Gandhi. ➤

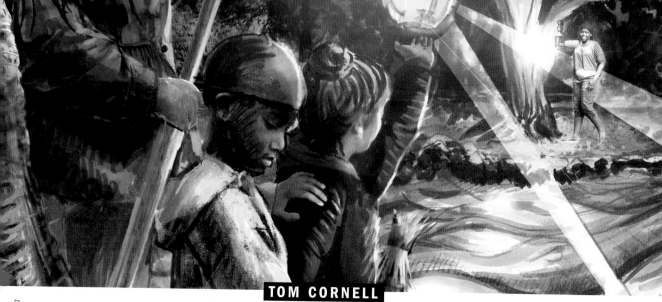

Photo by Steve Weinik www.muralarts.org

TOM CORNELL

The Future of Christian Nonviolence

Should Every Church Be a Peace Church?

Fifteen thousand US soldiers had already died in Vietnam when, on October 27, 1967, Father Philip Berrigan and three accomplices entered the Baltimore Selective Service headquarters carrying a pitcher of blood. Locating the cabinets containing the records of men eligible for the military draft, they poured the blood over the open files. The Baltimore Four, as they came to be known, were convicted six months later on felony charges. Days before they were to stand for sentencing, Philip Berrigan, together with his brother (and fellow Catholic priest) Daniel and seven others, entered the Selective Service offices in Catonsville, Maryland, hauled hundreds of draft files out onto an adjacent parking lot, and incinerated them using homemade napalm.

On hearing of the Berrigans' action, we at the Catholic Worker house in New York City were astounded by their escalation of tactics. Philip was a dear friend – he had baptized my daughter the year before – and now I admired his daring, wanting to believe that he had enlarged the boundaries of nonviolent action.

Not everyone was so enthusiastic. Dorothy Day, the radical pacifist founder of the Catholic Worker, while not condemning the Berrigans, remarked pointedly: "These acts are not ours." Property damage, in her view, was not part of the nonviolent arsenal. Burning one's own draft card was one thing – Dorothy herself had publicly urged young American men to do just that. But destroying other people's documents crossed a line.

Above, detail from We Rise! Children, Trauma, and Resilience. *This street mural from the City of Philadelphia Mural Arts Program was completed in 2013 with the participation of at-risk youth.*

Tom Cornell, a veteran peace activist and Catholic Worker, lives with his wife, Monica, at the Peter Maurin Farm in Marlboro, New York.

The Catonsville Nine, as they were called, received prison sentences of two to six years. The Berrigan brothers and three others refused to surrender and went underground. Dorothy considered this a major breach of nonviolent principles. She, together with other prominent pacifists who had re-launched the American peace movement after World War II, were committed to nonviolent direct action in the tradition of Mohandas Gandhi. This tradition required acting in "openness and truth" – including a willingness to stand before the courts and to accept whatever punishment they impose. The Berrigans did not agree.

Consistent with Dorothy's reservations, the *Catholic Worker* newspaper remained largely silent about the Catonsville action and the trial that followed, despite widespread coverage in the mainstream media. (An article in June 1968 was the lone exception.) And in the four decades that followed, we published virtually nothing on the Berrigans and the Plowshares movement that, in 1980, they would help launch. This brave and occasionally spectacular antiwar and antinuclear campaign remains a going concern to this day.

Forging Plowshares

In July 2012, three Plowshares activists including Sister Megan Rice, age eighty-two, broke into the Y-12 National Security Complex in Oak Ridge, Tennessee, which houses the world's biggest supply of enriched, weapons-grade uranium. Cutting through four perimeter fences, they reached the site's Protected Area without being apprehended, hammering on the uranium storage structure, pouring out human blood they had brought in baby bottles, and hanging banners and crime-scene tape.

The action garnered international attention, partly because it exposed the vulnerability of nuclear-weapons sites. Charged with federal felonies including sabotage, the three activists

remain in prison. Sister Megan, who is housed in a dormitory-style cell with sixty other prisoners, has become an eloquent advocate for her fellow inmates, to whom she ministers selflessly.

Yet are such Plowshares actions nonviolent? Within the peace movement, many think they are – the War Resisters League has awarded Plowshares its annual peace award. From the Christian point of view, weapons that are intended to kill the innocent may surely be destroyed in justice. Justice may even demand it. And on a personal level, many of the men and women involved in Plowshares activities have been Catholic Workers and beloved friends and comrades; like Sister Megan, several have paid a heavy price in long prison terms, which calls for respect.

But is it nonviolence? Is it disarmament? Disarmament occurs when people lay down their weapons, not when their weapons are taken from them. That only moves belligerents to procure more and better weapons if they can. When activists destroy weapons, do they effect any conversion or change of heart in their opponents? Do they lead any to lay down their arms? Are such actions what we need?

There are practical concerns as well. The secrecy involved in Plowshares activities invites infiltration by spies and agents provocateurs. Openness and truth must be laid aside. Secrecy breeds suspicion within the group and creates a class system of those "in the know," the "serious," and those who merely attend to chores or lend moral or financial support. This lack of transparency can lead to problems of moral coercion: Jim Forest, a fellow Catholic Worker, has written that he was motivated to join a draft-board raid largely in order to stay in the good graces of the Berrigan brothers. Again, is this nonviolent? A nonviolent army, after all, has no cannon fodder.

Many in the antinuclear movement have

literally put their lives on the line, risking being shot when they entered restricted areas. When Sister Megan was asked about these risks in an NPR interview, she answered that she was perfectly at peace with the possibility of being killed. Straight to heaven for her, no sweat! But how about the young security guard who might be obliged to shoot her? What of his mental and spiritual health after that?

What Is Christian Nonviolence?

The basis of Christian nonviolence is the same premise that underlies all of the church's social teaching: that every man, woman, and child is created in the image of God. Persons are never a means to an end; they are ends in themselves, and thus are not to be violated in any way, either in body, mind, or spirit. Persons are not disconnected individuals in a war of all against all, as in the capitalist model; nor are they to be subsumed into a larger whole, as in the collectivist model. Instead, all are formed in, by, and for community. Thus Pope John XXIII, in his 1963 encyclical, *Pacem in Terris,* grounded his hope for peace in human rights.

But how to establish and protect human rights? Most people throughout history have assumed this is only possible through physical force. An ancient Latin adage goes, *Si vis pacem, para bellum* – if you desire peace, prepare for war. That's like saying, "If you desire grapes, sow briars." Christian peacemakers would rather say, *Si vis pacem, para pacem* – if you desire peace, prepare for peace.

Christian nonviolence fits comfortably into the larger fabric of a more universal nonviolence. The US Catholic bishops acknowledged this when they cited Mohandas Gandhi along with Dorothy Day and Martin Luther King Jr. in their 1983 pastoral letter, *The Challenge of Peace.* Christian nonviolence takes a lesson from Hindu tradition in avoidance of harm, ahimsa, and in acknowledging the power

DOROTHY DAY

"Paperwork, cleaning the house, dealing with the innumerable visitors who come all through the day, answering the phone, keeping patience and acting intelligently, which is to find some meaning in all that happens – these things, too, are the works of peace."

from *The Catholic Worker,* Dec. 1965

of truth, satyagraha – "soul force," as King translated it.

Yet Christian nonviolence is also rooted in the gospel. It looks to the teachings of Jesus, the victory of the cross, the resurrection, and the witness of the church of the first three centuries, before the Constantinian accommodation. And it draws from a constant if submerged nonviolent tradition through subsequent ages: the witness of the Franciscans in the thirteenth century and since, the Quakers and Anabaptists from the seventeenth century to the present, and a minority of Catholics through the ages, even as the Just War tradition was dominant for fifteen hundred years.

An Alternative to War

Christian discipleship will be judged by the criteria of the Last Judgment: the works of mercy that Jesus describes in Matthew 25. As

Dorothy Day pointed out, war may be judged by these criteria too, for the works of war are the exact opposite of the works of mercy. Feed the hungry? No, destroy their crops! Give drink to the thirsty? No, poison their wells! Shelter the homeless? No, bomb their village! The weapons of Christian nonviolence include the spiritual works of mercy; again, the works of war are the exact opposite. Instruct the ignorant? No, lie to them! Counsel the doubtful? No, draft them or imprison them! Console the bereaved? Give them more deaths to grieve! Forgive injuries? Not on your life! Make them pay, ten times over!

Authentic nonviolence must be revolutionary because the social, political, economic order we live under violates the human person in fundamental ways – body, mind, and spirit. The present order is more accurately called disorder. It kills and maims the body by war and by withholding the means to life from the poor. It violates human intelligence because it thrives on lies – truth is always war's first casualty. And it violates the human conscience, which instinctively shrinks in horror from killing our own. As documented by Lt. Col. Dave Grossman, the West Point psychology professor who pioneered the conditioning technique known as killology, overcoming our natural aversion to homicide is a prime task of military training. Wars can be fought only by stilling the voice of conscience.

By contrast, nonviolence operates in transparency, openness, and truth. Nonviolence recognizes the humanity of the opponent and appeals to "that of God in everyone," as the Quakers put it – that which the Creator breathed into our first parents and which we all share, even the boss, the landlord, the racist, the oppressor, the warmonger. In struggle, the nonviolent activist does not seek victory but reconciliation, the redemption of the opponent, never his humiliation or annihilation. Therefore, the nonviolent activist always allows the opponent a way to retreat with dignity, an honorable way out of any conflict.

The principal weapon of nonviolence is dialogue. Genuine dialogue assumes the good faith of partners and avoids invidious language and ad hominem argument. Dialogue may be suspended at an impasse, but resumption is always a goal. The nonviolent armory includes protest, public dissent, noncooperation, and active resistance, but always with the purpose of re-establishing dialogue. Civil disobedience is the last weapon to be used, not the first, and should be undertaken after careful discernment under spiritual direction.

A Spiritual Discipline

Christian nonviolence is a way of life, not a tactic. Those who make the principles of nonviolence their own find that they change their way of working, of giving orders and taking them, of teaching, of preaching and ministering, of relating to spouses, children, elders, strangers, and friends as well as opponents. Often adopting nonviolence is part of a conversion process. The nonviolent activist is a man or woman of spiritual discipline, who has peace within, for one cannot give what one does not have.

In order to practice Christian nonviolence we have to prepare ourselves through study – nonviolence doesn't come naturally for most of us. Thomas Merton, the well-known author and Trappist monk, pointed to the superficiality of much of what he saw coming out of the peace movement of the 1960s: lack of clarity in the use of terms, shoddy thinking, and gratuitous assertion. If anything, the years since his death have seen worse. We Christians need to recover what our ancestors in the faith knew about peacemaking.

And we need a revolution of the heart. To purify our wills we need to pray. To tame our lusts we need self-control, discipline, and fasting in one way or another. Only then can we come to the study of nonviolence with the realistic hope of putting it into useful practice. One need not be a saint, but the intellectually slothful and the self-serving will not make effective nonviolent practitioners. The way of nonviolence must proceed person by person.

What about Defending the Innocent?

At this point, a reasonable objection confronts the pacifist. Jesus counsels that I turn my own cheek, not my neighbor's. Do we not have an obligation to protect the innocent? Does it not happen sometimes that the only effective way to protect the innocent is by force, even force of arms? Is it not a crime that cries to heaven that the international community did not intervene to stop the genocide in Rwanda and in Sudan?

Refusal to support military force in defense of the innocent for reasons of conscience does not extricate anyone from the moral dilemma. One response is to practice nonviolent action as an alternative. Advocates of nonviolence have pioneered peaceful ways to resist aggression or home-grown tyranny. Religious groups such as Maryknoll and the Quakers have long prepared for re-entry into conflict areas in Asia. Other groups such as Christian Peacemaker Teams and Voices for Creative Nonviolence have sent trained activists into conflict areas such as Iraq, Afghanistan, Israel/Palestine, and Central and South America as "accompaniment teams" to document abuses and to train others in the work of resistance and reconciliation.

Another response, suggested by Gandhi, is to build up community, creating "cells of good living" in a violent world. This is what Catholic Worker groups, the Bruderhof, and other intentional communities strive to do in ever increasing numbers. In these communities the poor and marginalized may be sheltered. According to Werner Jaeger, a classicist of the last century, such communities may play a crucial role in the re-ordering of society in

THOMAS MERTON

The First Step of Peacemaking

"All men seek peace first of all with themselves. That is necessary, because we do not naturally find rest even in our own being. We have to learn to commune with ourselves before we can communicate with other men and with God. A man who is not at peace with himself necessarily projects his interior fighting into the society of those he lives with, and spreads a contagion of conflict all around him. Even when he tries to do good to others his efforts are hopeless, since he does not know how to do good to himself. In moments of wildest idealism he may take it into his head to make other people happy, and in doing so he will overwhelm them with his own unhappiness. He seeks to find himself somehow in the work of making others happy. Therefore he throws himself into the work. As a result he gets out of the work all that he put into it: his own confusion, his own disintegration, his own unhappiness."   from *No Man Is an Island,* 1955

times of social disintegration; one need only recall how the monasteries preserved culture in Europe during the Dark Ages. The mission of these communities is "to build a new society within the shell of the old," words that appear in the 1905 constitution of the Industrial Workers of the World, authored by Thomas Haggerty, a Catholic priest.

All the same, there is weight to arguments for forceful intervention to protect the innocent. The innocent do need protection, and the world as we know it does need a police force. International police action is different from war. That is why, though I am a pacifist, I also believe there is a place for Just War thinking in Christian social teaching.

(Un)Just War

Just War theory was never intended as a framework by which war may be justified or as a means to deny the obvious meaning of the words of Jesus in the Gospels. Instead, it aspired to be a rational means for limiting war. It grapples with the questions: When is it justifiable to go to war (*jus ad bellum*)? What is permissible in warfare – are there any limits (*jus in bello*)? And what of the aftermath of victory – are there moral obligations that bind the victors (*jus post bellum*)?

Just War thinking evolved from attempts to answer these questions and to limit the destructiveness of warfare. Since it is based on reason rather than scripture, it belongs to the realm of moral philosophy, not theology. Though primarily associated with Catholic teaching going back to Augustine of Hippo, it has also been developed by Protestants, chief among them Hugo Grotius in the seventeenth century and Paul Ramsey of Princeton University in the twentieth.

According to a widely accepted definition, modern Just War theory holds that war may be resorted to: 1) under legitimate authority; 2) for sufficient reason; 3) with a just intention; 4) with reasonable expectation of success; and 5) as a last resort, all other options having been tried and failed. Once war has broken out, Just War theory requires that the means employed to fight it must be: 1) proportional, causing less evil than they remedy; and 2) careful to preserve civilian immunity, though Just War theory tolerates noncombatant deaths as "collateral damage" if they are not directly intended and if they are not causal to victory.

Is Just War Theory Meaningless?

What are Christian pacifists to make of Just War theory? Some have suggested that it should be entirely abandoned, on the grounds that it contradicts Jesus' clear teaching and has proven meaningless in practice. They have a point. Ever since Just War theory was invented, every side of every Western war has used its language to justify self-interested claims, and done so with ease. After all, no government has ever announced its intention to wage an unjust war. Never has it been observed that war planners, chiefs of state, and their cabinets met with their joint chiefs of staff to discuss how to apply Just War requirements to their agendas. No victorious nation has ever attributed its success to its own evil deeds, nor have its leaders ever been indicted by an international tribunal for war crimes. That happens only to losers.

Church leaders have had no better track record than the statesmen and generals. Throughout the ages, they have written a blank check to their governments on every side of virtually every war. (One exception came in 1971 when the US Catholic bishops judged the American war in Vietnam to be disproportionate in its evil effects, and therefore immoral. They did not, however, broadcast this decision with any clarity, vigor, or urgency.)

It might seem high time, then, to consign Just War theory to the scrap heap of church history, along with other discredited relics such as limbo for unbaptized infants. But this would be imprudent and premature, at the very least. Having put the Just War tradition aside, as some pacifists imagine they have done, they quickly reclaim its language whenever they criticize atrocities such as the targeting of civilians.

Consider the alternative to Just War theory: a world in which there are no limits on warfare even in theory, and in which what can be done may be done. This is clearly an amoral position, one that has proved dangerously attractive to some recent Christian thinkers. After the United States began to threaten preemptive war against Iraq in 2002, prominent Catholics such as Michael Novak and George Weigel argued for updating the Just War theory to allow for the Bush administration's actions. The problems with such opportunistic flexibility are obvious.

The Just War tradition thus remains a crucial measuring stick. This is true not just for its adherents, but also for pacifists seeking to discern how to respond to a given war. Not all wars are equal, and pacifists' choice of response – ranging from protest to noncoopera- tion, obstruction, and even sabotage – may depend on the degree of injustice perpetrated by the war-makers. During World War II, for instance, the pacifist movement in America generally did not attempt to impede the war effort, implicitly recognizing the element of justice in the Allies' cause. Dorothy Day, for one, protested the killing, especially the bombing of civilians. With A. J. Muste and the historic peace churches such as the Mennonites, Quakers, and Brethren, she urged young men to refuse military service. Yet she did not attempt to block arms shipments.

Every Church a Peace Church?

Just War theory has far more to offer pacifists than a useful tool. It can become a path to the abolition of war. An extreme speculation? Not if we take the Just War criteria seriously. What- ever we may make of the near total absence of Christians in the military before AD 313, and however we may evaluate conditions in past ages, in the present day war almost certainly

cannot be defended as a last resort, nor can it be waged in a proportionate manner and with respect for civilian immunity. In other words, modern war by its nature is not just, nor can it be. That is why the Catholic Church is becom- ing, if not pacifist, then at least a peace church. Other major Christian communions are on a similar journey.

Already in 1947, Cardinal Alfredo Ottaviani wrote that war has changed *in specie*, in its very nature, and must be altogether forbidden. He would prove not to be an outlier. Pope John XXIII, in *Pacem in Terris*, taught that "it is contrary to reason to hold that war is any longer a suitable way to restore violated rights." And the Second Vatican Council unequivo- cally condemned the use of weapons of mass destruction, urging Catholics to consider questions of war and peace "with an entirely new attitude" (*Gaudium et Spes*).

> **The Catholic Church is becoming, if not pacifist, then at least a peace church.**

Imagine solid ranks of Cath- olic conscientious objectors heeding the call of Pope Paul VI at the United Nations on October 4, 1965: "No more war, war never again!" His message was echoed by Pope John Paul II when he addressed the youth of Ireland at Drogheda in 1979: "On my knees I beg you to turn from the paths of violence and return to the ways of peace. . . . Violence only delays the day of justice. Violence destroys the work of justice. . . . Do not follow any leaders who train you in the ways of inflicting death. Love life! Respect life, in yourselves and in others. Give yourselves to the service of life, not the service of death. . . . Violence is the enemy of justice. Only peace can lead the way to true justice."

In his 1991 encyclical, *Centesimus Annus,* John Paul II again pleaded, "No, never again war, which destroys the lives of innocent people, teaches how to kill, throws into upheaval even the lives of those who do the killing and leaves behind a trail of resentment and hatred, thus making it all the more difficult to find a just solution of the very problems that provoked the war."

And Pope Benedict XVI has said: "I would like to call out to the consciences of those who form part of armed groups of any kind. To each and every one, I say: Stop, reflect, and abandon the path of violence!" (Angelus message, Jan. 1, 2010). And more: "It is impossible to interpret Jesus as a violent person. Violence is contrary to the kingdom of God; it is a tool of the Antichrist. Violence never serves humanity, but dehumanizes" (Angelus message, Mar. 11, 2012).

Let us hear no more, "Yes, but . . ."

Christians must be at the vanguard of the war against war.

When war is outlawed, as it must be if humanity is to survive its penchant for self-destruction, our progeny will look back on justifications for war with the shame we do today on justifications for slavery by Christian theologians a mere one hundred and fifty years ago. If Christians are not in the vanguard of the war against war, if that is left to nonbelievers, then we will have deserted the field, cowards indeed, and other generations, if there be any, will have to restore the credibility of the gospel of the Prince of Peace and the integrity of his church.

Disarmament must be a top priority. Most people would agree in principle – popes and presidents included – but there is no will to do it. It's been over fifty years since we had a broad-based disarmament movement in the United States or the world. Meanwhile the nuclear threat has only become more severe as nuclear-weapons capability proliferates.

In their 1983 letter, *The Challenge of Peace,* the US Catholic bishops challenged the nuclear deterrent, calling it morally acceptable only temporarily and conditionally, to buy time for multilateral nuclear disarmament. But that time has already run out, according to the Vatican, which already called for the universal abolition of nuclear weapons in 1997. More recently, Cardinal Renato Martino, President of the Pontifical Council for Justice and Peace, has gone even further: "Individuals and communities have the duty to express clearly their complete and radical rejection of all forms of violence, especially that fueled in God's holy name" (*Zenit*, Feb. 19, 2007).

So we have calls for disarmament from the Vatican itself! In the Catholic Church, a grassroots peace movement among the laity has been growing – and not just among the usual suspects in the Catholic Worker, Pax Christi, and Plowshares movements. Academic groups such as the Kroc Institute at the University of Notre Dame are contributing too.

Even more Christians must rise to meet the challenge. As Thomas Merton wrote: "The duty of the Christian in this [present] crisis is to strive with all his power and intelligence, with his faith, his hope in Christ and love for God and man, to do the one task which God has imposed upon us in the world today. That task is to work for the total abolition of war" (*The Catholic Worker*, Oct. 1961).

So let us get to work. The first words I ever heard from Dorothy Day, sixty-one years ago, were, "There are great things that have to be done, and who will do them but the young?" No cause is more noble or more necessary. Pray and study first, then get out there and start moving. ⤳

Nonviolence: An Impossible Ideal?

A Reading from Dietrich Bonhoeffer

Seventy years ago, the martyr Dietrich Bonhoeffer was killed in the Flossenbürg concentration camp on Hitler's orders. Today he is often lionized as a hero of the armed resistance to Nazism – perhaps too uncritically (see our Summer 2014 issue). Wherever the biographical truth may lie, Bonhoeffer's passionate call for Christian nonviolence cannot be just passed over. He asks us: Are we ready to take up our cross as Jesus did, or not?

You have heard that it was said, "An eye for an eye and a tooth for a tooth." But I say to you, do not resist an evildoer. But if anyone strikes you on the right cheek, turn the other also; and if anyone wants to sue you and take your coat, give your cloak as well; and if anyone forces you to go one mile, go also the second mile. Give to everyone who begs from you, and do not refuse anyone who wants to borrow from you. (Matt. 5:38–42)

The right way to requite evil, according to Jesus, is not to resist it.

We are concerned not with evil in the abstract, but with the evil *person*. Jesus bluntly calls the evil person evil. If I am assailed, I am not to condone or justify aggression. Patient endurance of evil does not mean a recognition of its rights. That is sheer sentimentality, and Jesus will have nothing to do with it. The shameful assault, the deed of violence, and the act of exploitation are still evil. The disciple must realize this, and bear witness to it as Jesus did, just because this is the only way evil can be met and overcome. The very fact that the evil which assaults him is unjustifiable makes it imperative that he should not resist it, but play it out and overcome it by patiently enduring the evil person. Suffering willingly endured is stronger than evil; it spells death to evil.

There is no deed on earth so outrageous as to justify a different attitude. The worse the evil, the readier must the Christian be to suffer; he

*Above:
Antonello
da Messina,
detail from
Crucifixion*

From Dietrich Bonhoeffer, "Revenge," in The Cost of Discipleship, *trans. R. H. Fuller (SCM Press, 1959).*

must let the evil person fall into Jesus' hands.

The Reformers . . . distinguished between personal sufferings and those incurred by Christians in the performance of duty as bearers of an office ordained by God, maintaining that the precept of nonviolence applies to the first but not to the second. In the second case we are not only freed from obligation to eschew violence, but if we want to act in a genuine spirit of love we must do the very opposite, and meet force with force in order to check the assault of evil. It was along these lines that the Reformers justified war and other legal sanctions against evil. But this distinction between person and office is totally alien to the teaching of Jesus. He says nothing about that. He addresses his disciples as men who have left all to follow him, and the precept of nonviolence applies equally to private life and official duty. He is the Lord of all life, and demands undivided allegiance. Furthermore, when it comes to practice, this distinction raises insoluble difficulties. Am I ever acting only as a private person or only in an official capacity? If I am attacked am I not at once the father of my children, the pastor of my flock, and e.g. a government official? Am I not bound for that very reason to defend myself against every attack, for reason of responsibility to my office? And am I not also always an individual, face to face with Jesus, even in the performance of my official duties? Am I not therefore obliged to resist every attack just because of my responsibility for my office? Is it right to forget that the follower of Jesus is always utterly alone, always the individual, who in the last resort can only decide and act for himself? Don't we act most responsibly on behalf of those entrusted to our care if we act in this aloneness?

How then can the precept of Jesus be justified in the light of experience? It is obvious that weakness and defenselessness only invite aggression. Is then the demand of Jesus nothing but an impracticable ideal? Does he refuse to face up to realities – or shall we say, to the sin of the world? There may of course be a legitimate place for such an ideal in the inner life of the Christian community, but in the outside world such an ideal appears to wear the blinkers of perfectionism and to take no account of sin. Living as we do in a world of sin and evil, we can have no truck with anything as impracticable as that.

Jesus, however, tells us that it is just *because* we live in the world, and just *because* the world is evil, that the precept of nonresistance must be put into practice. Surely we do not wish to accuse Jesus of ignoring the reality and power of evil! Why, the whole of his life was one long conflict with the devil. He calls evil evil, and that is the very reason why he speaks to his followers in this way. How is that possible?

If we took the precept of nonresistance as an ethical blueprint for general application, we should indeed be indulging in idealistic dreams: we should be dreaming of a utopia with laws which the world would never obey. To make nonresistance a principle for secular life is to deny God by undermining his gracious ordinance for the preservation of the world. But Jesus is no draftsman of political blueprints; he is the one who vanquished evil through suffering. It looked as though evil had triumphed on the cross, but the real victory belonged to Jesus. And the cross is the only justification for the precept of nonviolence, for it alone can kindle a faith in the victory over evil which will enable people to obey that precept. Only such obedience is blessed with the promise that we shall be partakers of Christ's victory as well as of his sufferings. . . .

The cross is the only power in the world which proves that suffering love can avenge and vanquish evil.

Is Pacifism Enough?

EBERHARD ARNOLD

Germany, 1934. Eighteen months after Hitler's rise to power, Plough's founding editor warned of the threat of a second major war – and foresaw that the international peace movement, which he had championed, would be powerless to stop it. His reflections remain unsettlingly relevant today.

Does pacifism suffice? I don't think it is enough. When over a thousand people have been killed unjustly, without trial, under Hitler's new government, isn't that already war? When hundreds of thousands of people in concentration camps are robbed of their freedom and stripped of all dignity, isn't that war? When in China and Russia millions starve to death while in other countries millions of tons of wheat are stockpiled, isn't that war? When thousands of women prostitute their bodies and ruin their lives for the sake of money, isn't that war? When millions of babies are murdered by abortion each year, isn't that war? When people are forced to work like slaves because they cannot otherwise feed their children, isn't that war? When the wealthy live in villas surrounded by parks while other families don't even have a single room to themselves, isn't that war? When some people build up enormous bank accounts while others earn scarcely enough for basic necessities, isn't that war? When reckless drivers kill tens of thousands of people each year, isn't that war?

We do not advocate a pacifism that believes it can prevent future war. This claim is not valid; there is war right up to the present day. We do not represent a pacifism that believes in the elimination of war through the restraining influence of certain superior nations. We do not agree with a pacifism that ignores the root causes of war – private property and capitalism – and tries to bring about peace in the midst of social injustice. We have no faith in the pacifism held by businessmen who beat down their competitors, nor do we believe in a pacifism whose amiable representatives cannot live in peace with their own spouses.

Since there are so many kinds of pacifism we cannot believe in, we would rather not use the word *pacifism* at all. But we are friends of peace, and we want to help bring about peace. Jesus said, "Blessed are the peacemakers!"

If we really want peace, we must represent it in all areas of life. We cannot injure love in any way or for any reason. So we cannot kill anyone; we cannot harm anyone economically; we cannot take part in a system that establishes lower standards of living for manual workers than for academics. We must spurn anything that breeds hatred or oppression.

In other words, we must live like Jesus. He helped everyone in body and soul. Our whole life must be dedicated to love.

From Eberhard Arnold, talks on August 9 and 17, 1934, translated by Gladys Mason.

Detail from a street mural by Icy and Sot, stencil artists originally from Tabriz, Iran, in Williamsburg, Brooklyn (on South 6 by the bridge). *www.icyandsot.com*

Disruptive Peacemaking
Living Out God's Impossible Standard

ETHAN HUGHES

Above: Candlesticks with home-made beeswax candles stand ready for use at Still Waters Sanctuary.

Ethan Hughes was thirteen when his father was killed by a drunk driver. When he later learned that thirty million people have died in automobile accidents – and after he witnessed a massive oil spill in the Amazon rainforest – he vowed he wouldn't drive a car. Biking was but the first step on a road to radical simplicity that has since caught the imagination of thousands.

Eight years ago my wife Sarah and I moved to La Plata, Missouri, and began a full-time attempt at peacemaking on an eighty-acre homestead. Our community's name is Still Waters Sanctuary, taking inspiration from Psalm 23: "He leads me beside still waters; he restores my soul."

Since then, over ten thousand seekers from all over the world have visited us to experience a life without tractors, chainsaws, power tools, computers, televisions, smartphones, and most consumer goods and services. We strive to live free of electricity and petroleum products. If that sounds like we're missing out, we are not. Instead, we're blessed with goats, cows, chickens, ducks, bees, mushroom logs, and a herb garden. Our life includes weaving, spinning, hide tanning, canning and drying produce, and grinding grain with a pedal-powered mill. We grow food without chemicals and machines, offer our produce and hospitality without charge, and build our homes by hand with natural, local materials. We travel by

Photograph courtesy of Katie Currid

bicycle, illuminate with beeswax candles, play live music, dine on wild edibles, and haul trees with horses. Life starts at sunrise with an hour of morning prayer before we move out into creation to get to work.

We're also committed to serving in nursing homes and homeless shelters in our local community. And when our hearts call us to struggle for justice, we also occasionally practice civil disobedience and spend nights in jail. We try to live in the spirit of Wendell Berry's words: "If we are serious about peace, then we must work for it as ardently, seriously, continuously, carefully, and bravely as we have ever prepared for war."

Why Live Simply?

As peacemakers, we strive to understand the roots of war: greed, consumerism, fear, slavery, and power over others. These feed off each other. If we are attached to goods, we will have to defend them or have others defend them

for us. Fear and greed lead us to start locking our doors, putting up surveillance systems, and hoarding our treasures on earth. If we call the police to deal with theft, we call upon the violent empire we are trying to move away from, since the police and military both use coercion and lethal weapons to maintain order.

To be peacemakers we must systematically remove the seeds of war from every part of our life. In the 1760s, the Quaker leader John Woolman gave up certain belongings of his – a chair, dyed clothing, a silver cup, and sugar – when he realized that their production fueled war and slavery. Woolman challenges us to test "whether the seeds of war have any nourishment in these our possessions."

Having excess is a form of war. While some people have ten times more resources than they need, others are wandering cold, homeless, and hungry. Saint Basil declares, "You with a second coat in your closet, it does not belong to you.

Community members gather for a shared meal. Because there is no refrigerator, the cooks carefully estimate the amounts so that no food goes to waste.

Ethan Hughes and his wife Sarah founded Still Waters Sanctuary, a community seeking to live out a "gift economy" that doesn't rely on money. To get in touch, contact Still Waters Sanctuary, 28408 Frontier Lane, La Plata, Missouri 63549.

Draft horses replace tractors for farming, and are rewarded with access to ample pasture.

You have stolen it from the poor one who is shivering in the cold."

Living simply means resisting the comfort and efficiency that industrial society offers us at the expense of the environment. Almost every act in modern society destroys or fouls God's creation: flushing the toilet, turning on a light, sipping coffee shipped across the world, buying goods made of plastic, and using fossil fuels and household cleaners. Wendell Berry writes, "Our destruction of nature is not just bad steward-ship, or stupid economics, or a betrayal of family responsibility. . . . It is flinging God's gifts into God's face."

Whenever we place our faith in mammon, wealth, and things, we enter a state of war with ourselves, with each other, with creation, and with God. The cycle feeds itself, gaining momentum as long as it goes unchecked. We must disrupt it at all costs. Any act of peacemak-ing is disruptive to a society built around war.

Working with Our Hands

How do we move in this direction? Lanza del Vasto (1901–1981), a student of Gandhi, offers us a simple formula: "Work with your hands. Don't

force others to work for you. Don't make others into slaves, even if you call them paid workers. Find the shortest, simplest way between the earth, the hands, and the mouth. . . . When you have to sweat to satisfy your needs, you soon know whether it is worth your while. But if it is someone else's sweat, there is no end to our needs. . . . Do it yourself. Show that it is possible to live this way."

Del Vasto himself sought to live out this vision. In 1948 he founded the Community of the Ark at La Borie Noble, France. This com-munity, where Sarah and I lived for eighteen months before starting in Missouri, is the inspiration for our imperfect experiment at Still Waters Sanctuary.

At the Community of the Ark, the day was punctuated by prayer and song, and a bell of mindfulness that rang to invite everyone to stop their labor and ground themselves in the pres-ence of God. Decisions were made collectively by consensus. We sat on handmade furniture, spent evenings by candlelight, watched members spin and weave their clothing, helped host thousands of visitors, and ate food grown organically by horse and human power. We helped put up three tons of potatoes, three tons of wheat, and 1500 quarts of tomatoes, and we helped milk seven cows for cheese, butter, and cream. With hand tools we cut and split the firewood that heated our homes and water.

All members of the Ark take a vow of poverty and live below the taxable income level, and so do not have to pay war taxes. Once a year, at the feast of Saint Michael, the Ark also gives away all the money in its coffers.

This was the closest thing to the Peaceable Kingdom that we have ever experienced. We witnessed a new society built on faith and sharing, not on riches and possessions. We saw the Sermon on the Mount lived out: "Do not worry, saying 'What will we eat?' or 'What will we wear?' . . . but strive first for the kingdom of God and his righteousness, and these things will be given to you as well" (Matt. 6:31–33). At the Ark, our lives did not require wars for oil and materials from across the world, oppressive labor, pollution, and the killing of creation. Work with our hands was a prayer to God, and the seeds of war were removed from our lives.

Challenges in Peacemaking

There are social and political risks in taking God's will for peace seriously. If we are called to live like Jesus and the early Christians, we must pray for the love that casts out all fear. We are called to name, unmask,

and resist the systemic evils that cause war, and to stop cooperating with all unjust social structures. To avoid this call, many Christians have chosen safer and less disruptive practices, such as charity. Charity is a wonderful thing, but we cannot pretend it will eliminate the seeds of war.

How do we know that we have been disruptive with our peacemaking? Some of us here have been jailed for blocking roads to nuclear weapons plants and fracking stations. We have had death threats because of our peace witness during wartime. We have been verbally attacked and ridiculed for our simple lifestyle.

Besides these outer challenges, of course, there are inner challenges as well. Despite our efforts to live peacefully, we at Still Waters Sanctuary still experience discord, anger, jealousy, sexism, racism, fear, and greed on a daily basis. Some days it seems I cannot muster the love necessary to be patient with my children. Other days I treat my beloved wife with contempt and belittlement.

For those of us pursuing radical simplicity, it's all too easy to judge others – a temptation we must face and firmly reject. We also experience daily how we are still connected to the systems of waste, pollution, and destruction, despite our best efforts to build a peaceful world. While at the Ark, too, we experienced similar hypocrisies, paradoxes, and shortcomings. Shall we give

"Much more than going into the street . . . the most efficient action and the most significant testimony in favor of nonviolence and truth is living: living a life that is one, where everything goes in the same sense, from prayer and meditation to laboring for our daily bread, from the teaching of the doctrine to the making of manure, from cooking to singing and dancing around the fire; living a life in which there is no violence or unfairness. . . . What matters is to show that such a life is possible and even not more difficult than a life of gain, nor more unpleasant than a life of pleasure, nor less natural than an 'ordinary' life."

Lanza del Vasto, *Warriors of Peace*, 1974

The author's daughter Etta rides on her father's back in the community dining room. Fun and celebration – expressing gratitude for the joy of life – are a vital part of the community's vision.

up because of our failures? We believe we must all keep climbing the steep mountain toward God's peaceable kingdom.

Bearing Fruit

Despite our flawed attempt to live out peace and justice, over the past eight years Still Waters Sanctuary has nurtured the birth of autonomous sister communities and experiments in rural California, inner-city Reno, and Kansas City. Other groups are in the process of finding land. We created the Possibility Alliance to link all of these experiments in peacemaking and integral nonviolence.

Still Waters is also the headquarters of the Bicycling Superheroes, a seven hundred–strong organization that responds to calls for help from around the country. Dressed as superheroes, we get on our bikes and ride to where someone needs a hand. So far we've been led to inner-city Detroit, to areas hit by Hurricane Katrina, and to twenty-six states and seven countries.

Closer to home, the White Rose Catholic Worker Farm, the Peace and Permaculture Education Center, and a land-trust community of three off-grid homesteads have all moved next door to our community. We feel blessed with all of this fruit, but still have no idea where God is leading us next.

We believe we are called to try to live out this seemingly unattainable request from God. We believe we must apply all of our gifts, strengths, resources, and lives to these tasks, and that our striving will bring us closer to God's great goal. We pray for God's grace so that there may be peace in our hearts and on earth. As Thomas à Kempis reminds us, "Love feels no burden, thinks nothing of trouble, attempts what is above its strength, pleads no excuse of impossibility." ⤳

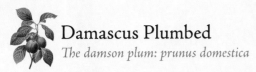

Damascus Plumbed
The damson plum: prunus domestica

In quiet hedgerows, down aimless village lanes,
clingstones, their origin, till now, in doubt,
post-rationing neglected on the bough,
hang down in droves, to drop, like severed heads,
decay. Giant sloes, their genes unbound, ink flicks
from hapless pens, blunt arrowheads, egg-shaped
lead weights, these flawless jewels against the green,
slate blue to deepest indigo, tear drupes,
hint of the orient, sweet damascene.
Though flawless raw – in Syria, one dry
sour note round here's pure gall. First fuse of firm
lime flesh, cheeks wither in surprise. Appalled,
what makes great jam bad med'cine unconfined,
we swallow, blink through tearful, childish eyes.

PETER BRANSON

Fiddlesticks
Pteridium: common bracken

Downsbanks, the Outlanes, near Stone, Staffs

Good uses once, bad press the enemy
these days: relentless mobster, triffid from
some darker world, a ticking toxic bomb;
giant smotherer, hair-trigger *fiddlehead*,
sea horse, palms microdots by sleight-of-hand,
lust-primed, on lacy fronds; full-cocking, fires
live dust; now toasted, humming, texture, taste
and smell, green shoots quick underground, makes rust.
We charge, 'The True-Born Englishman' our text,
resist your flaxen horde, outlandish waves
of 'kern and gallowglass, invasive tides
of migrants, infidels, with garden canes,
then heroes, glorious in retreat, course home
on armored steeds, peckish, sun-flushed, replete.

PETER BRANSON

The Blessings of Conflict

PEACEMAKING WITHIN COMMUNITY

CHARLES E. MOORE

Dale, a man in my church, showed up one day to a Bible study I was leading on the Sermon on the Mount. Within minutes, he raised objections to my take on Jesus' teaching. When I tried to respond, he appeared satisfied, and the next week he showed up again, this time with a couple of his buddies. But almost before we began, the arguments started flying. Soon Dale was accusing me of teaching a false, socialistic gospel. I ended the session earlier than usual, and afterward suggested to Dale that he find some other Bible study to attend. He stormed out.

A few days later Dale asked to meet me for lunch. Was this a setup? I hated conflict. Would the ranting continue? But our meeting began in a surprising way. Dale apologized for his behavior – he felt bad for being a disturbance, though it was clear he still thought I was off-base. Then he went on to talk about his past: how his father had been blown to bits in Vietnam, how his mother drank herself to death, how he managed to put himself through college on an ROTC scholarship, and how he proudly served in the Army for four years. At one point in the conversation, his eyes welled up and he looked at me with a helpless, boyish expression. He told me that I didn't have to worry about him coming around anymore and abruptly said he had to go. I never saw Dale again.

A couple of years later I decided to move to Denver's inner city with some friends from seminary. We started working with a nearby church ministry that provided people on the street a kind of living room that served free coffee day and night. Joe, the pastor of the church, didn't appreciate our growing presence. It didn't take long before we were accused of stealing sheep. In the face-to-face confrontation that followed, Joe wouldn't budge, and

Charles E. Moore is a member of the Bruderhof community in Esopus, New York, and editor of Christoph Friedrich Blumhardt's Everyone Belongs to God, *a new book from Plough (see page 70).*

neither would Paul, one of the members of our household. So Paul skipped town to start another ministry, leaving the rest of us to fend for ourselves.

As I got to know Joe, I learned that he was a victim of the 1960s drug culture. He had not only stoned himself into a semi-permanent stupor, he also started to hear voices. He decided to live in a teepee in the foothills on Denver's outskirts to become a hermit. He had gone insane, he told me, and might well have died but for his parents' intervention. Joe's conversion to Jesus, however, led him out of insanity. It also brought him among the emotionally dysfunctional people who lived under bridges and in the back alleys of Denver's "skid row." He admitted that he was still battling the voices, but the voices now lived in society's rejected and abandoned. He was now their defender; they were his sheep.

My encounters with Dale and Joe got me thinking more about conflict and what to do about it. I had learned as a child to avoid any kind of friction at all possible costs. Dad exploded one too many times, so I learned to hide. I tried everything I could to eliminate conflict in my life. But I soon found that this would not be possible if I hoped to have meaningful and lasting relationships, the kind I read about in the New Testament church.

If avoiding conflict was not the answer, and neither was a winner-take-all style of confrontation, then what was the answer? It gradually dawned on me that though conflict is inevitable, it isn't irredeemable. Jesus not only came into a world ridden with conflict, but he also shows us how it can be overcome. Because of conflict we can know the blessedness of being peacemakers. Because we hurt each other we can practice Jesus' command to forgive seventy times seven. Because of our differences we can come to know real unity. Christ shows us how instead of avoiding conflict, or escalating its damages, we can follow him through it.

In *Our Journey Home,* Jean Vanier writes, "Community life can become a real school for growth and love; it reveals differences – differences which irritate or are painful; it reveals the wounds and shadows inside us, the plank in our own eye, our capacity for judging and rejecting others, the difficulty we have in listening to and accepting others. These difficulties can lead people to run away from community . . . or lead them to work on themselves and understand and serve others and their needs better."

Relationships by their very nature breed conflict. But in Christ, conflict is a school in which love can be tested and refined, where we learn to forgive and be forgiven, and where the illusions we have of ourselves can come into the light and be transformed.

Several years ago my wife and I were helping to oversee a fledgling community in Albany, New York. Living quarters were tight, the tasks endless, and the personalities of the twenty individuals differed widely. I kept butting heads with a fellow member, James, who was several years older than me. Our conflicts mostly revolved around practical matters. One day I blew up. James simply didn't do what we had agreed on regarding the fencing project in our backyard. I had had enough.

But instead of walking away, we committed ourselves to working things through. We were bound to make good our pledge to always place Christ's honor above being in the right. In the process, we got to know each other as we really were. I saw anew how my need for control was not only unhealthy but stood in the way of true camaraderie. James shared how much he suffered under a fear of authority, but that he didn't want that fear to be an obstacle to our life together. Amid conflict we found each other's hearts, and the wall that had stood between us came tumbling down.

When we avoid conflict or abandon those who become a source of pain, we miss out on becoming the kind of community that can help us change. By selectively distancing ourselves from others, by always keeping our relational options open and fluid, we perpetuate the lie that conflict is an evil to be avoided. But by embracing conflict we learn that the brokenness that exists in others most assuredly also resides in us, and that Christ can heal the pain we all share.

Of course, conflict by itself is not automatically redemptive. There must be some common understanding and mutual commitment. Conflict is like fire: it can purify us, or it can destroy us. The outcome depends on how seriously we take Jesus' words: "First go and be reconciled to your brother or sister; then come and offer your gift on the altar." "If your brother sins against you, go and point out his fault, just between the two of you." We are called to a way that transcends the typical responses of fight or flight. Christ's way is the hard way of mutual correction, of going directly to each other in humility and love, of turning to others for help.

Our deepest craving is to love and be loved – yet it's one we attain not by a decision of the will, but rather through allowing Christ to lift the obstacles separating us from our neighbor. When we choose the way of the cross, where Christ's body is broken, and place it above our hurt feelings, inadequacies, and stubborn egos, then conflict can purge out the concealed offal in our lives. We can experience the Wounded Healer himself, the one who meets us in the pain and fears of our brother and sister. ⤳

PEACE PILGRIM

*N*o one walks so safely as one who walks humbly and harmlessly with great love and great faith. For such a person gets through to the good in others (and there is good in everyone), and therefore cannot be harmed. This works between individuals, it works between groups, and it would work between nations if nations had the courage to try it.

For twenty-eight years, Mildred Lisette Norman Ryder (1908–1981), known as "Peace Pilgrim," crisscrossed America on foot to share her simple message: "Overcome evil with good, falsehood with truth, and hatred with love." She had one set of clothing, carried no money, and only ate when food was offered. After 25,000 miles she stopped counting and kept walking.

ALBERT SCHWEITZER

*W*e live in a time when the good faith of peoples is doubted more than ever before. Expressions throwing doubt on the trustworthiness of each other are bandied back and forth. . . . We cannot continue in this paralyzing mistrust. If we want to work our way out of the desperate situation in which we find ourselves, another spirit must enter into the people. . . . We must approach them in the spirit that we are human beings, all of us, and that we feel ourselves fitted to feel with each other; to think and will together in the same way.

By age thirty Albert Schweitzer (1875–1965) was already an acclaimed organist, pastor, and scholar. But the lack of medical care in Africa convinced him to devote the rest of his life to serving the people there as a physician. In 1913 he and his wife Hélène opened a hospital in present-day Gabon, where he worked until his death at age ninety. Schweitzer was awarded the 1952 Nobel Peace Prize.

Sources: Peace Pilgrim, *Peace Pilgrim: Her Life and Work in Her Own Words* (Ocean Tree Books, 1982), 31. Albert Schweitzer, *Peace or Atomic War?* (Henry Holt, 1958), 44.

From Small Seeds, Great Things Grow

A sharecropper's son starts a community garden to save young lives.

RICHARD JOYNER

In 2005 I realized that too many people were dying young in my home town of Conetoe, North Carolina. In one year alone, I officiated at the funerals of thirty congregants under the age of thirty-two. Many of the deaths were health-related: poor diets, no exercise. Nearly two-thirds of the congregation were obese. It started to feel unconscionable to me to see someone one hundred pounds overweight on Sunday morning and not say anything about it. Then they'd die of a heart attack and we'd have another funeral. Although I had been a minister for a quarter century – nearly half my life – only now did I see that my pulpit went beyond the church.

Only a third of the adults had jobs. Most didn't have insurance and lived in poverty. I wanted to find a way to lift up my community and improve its members' mental, physical, and economic health.

Conetoe is a little town in an area once filled with cotton plantations. It has long been a "food desert": fresh vegetables were rarely available, and even when they were, people couldn't afford them. I realized we could grow fresh, healthy food for ourselves. That's when we started the Community Garden and Family Life Center, which began as a summer school program to grow healthy food and keep the children physically active.

Farming may sound romantic to some, but it was a painful hardship for me growing up. I was one of thirteen children in a sharecropping family, which meant doing work for another

man's gain. I will never forget my father's face when he was underpaid by the farm boss. He was unable to respond to the injustice because he knew the consequences for his family. Farms would hire him because he had all these children – thirteen males, including my brothers and boy cousins – and time after time I watched him struggle against poverty and my mother's disappointment. I saw him turn away to avoid my mother's eyes, and her anger. That life was not for me.

I am a carbon copy of my father, but I tried to escape his fate by joining the army after high school, serving overseas in Germany. I loved the structure and the sense of order, and when I came home I enlisted in the National Guard. In 2001 I was called to serve the church in Conetoe, and I returned to build a future in a place that had long held many sorrows for me.

Starting our own garden in Conetoe meant that the fruits of our labors would be our own.

It was a chance to rewrite that old story into something new and hopeful, but I had to confront old memories that were easier to forget.

Now nearly a decade has passed since we started our garden, which feeds our community in body and soul. It began with two acres of land donated by members of the community, and now has grown to fifteen farm plots around the county. The largest is twenty-five acres, with four fields, two greenhouses, and about 150 beehives. The young people do the hard work, taught by their elders, who have their own stories of sharecropping and of the family gardens that used to mean the difference between hunger and a full belly.

We have afterschool and summer camp programs that teach the children to plan, plant, and harvest the produce, which they then sell at farmers' markets, on roadside stands, and to restaurants. We gather honey from our hives and sell it or share it with our low-income

Rev. Richard Joyner is pastor of the Conetoe Chapel Missionary Baptist Church in North Carolina, where he also serves as a hospital chaplain and heads the Conetoe Family Life Center and Community Garden. He is a 2014 winner of The Purpose Prize, which honors social innovators over age sixty.

neighbors. While much of the produce stays within the community, we've also been growing a business, which now makes around $5000 a year. We raise and sell seedlings to individuals and businesses, and our honey is on supermarket shelves seventy-five miles away, in Raleigh. The money goes to school supplies and scholarships. Now that more of our youth are graduating from high school and going on to college, it's been put to good use.

You can see the change happen. And it's a change that lasts.

Adults donate time to help with homework, transportation, and the garden work. Everyone participates in Healthy Sunday suppers, where healthy, garden-grown food is cooked and served by the youngsters in "right-sized" portions.

Season by season, Conetoe is growing healthier and stronger. Many people have lost weight. We've seen fewer visits to the emergency room and, thankfully, fewer deaths.

People from outside Conetoe are asking us what we've done. We are one of several churches participating in a study of diabetes and heart disease being conducted by The Brody School of Medicine at East Carolina University, which has verified the health improvements over time. Churches in twenty-one counties are using our model to build their own community gardens, sowing the seeds of good health one row, one acre, one field at a time. That's the lesson which is important to share: this work took time to build and grow, but over time, it has become the center of our community, and a source of physical and spiritual sustenance. Everyone has a role, everyone has a voice, and everyone can make a difference.

Our young people take pride in their work, and that pride shows in how tall they stand and how they speak. When an older member of the community gives a child a blessing – placing her hands on that child's head with the prayer that the child grows strong and does good in the world – you can see the change happen. And it's a change that lasts.

Now in my sixties, I am still healing from my youth. Seeing the young people learn and have fun while farming has redeemed the humiliation I felt as a sharecropper's son. I don't know when I'm going to die, but I know I'm not going to go with all the anger I once held inside me.

A few years ago a child in our community stole money from the church. Some of the congregants wanted to press charges to teach him a lesson, but we decided to ask our young people to handle the matter. A bunch of teenagers from Conetoe talked to the prosecutor and the youth was sentenced to community service in the garden. Today his life is back on track. He is in community college and I see him in church almost every Sunday.

The moral leadership the kids showed is an antidote to the pain and negativity they could be carrying around. Just as our young people learn from us, we learn from them. Together we get closer to the spiritual, physical, and economic healing that I dreamed of ten years ago when we planted our first garden.

Artwork by Lisa Toth

The Legend of Heliopher

A Tale by Maxim Gorky

Retold by Hardy Arnold

ONCE UPON A TIME there was a race that was lost in a great, dark forest. The trees stood so close together that the light of the sun could not penetrate the thickly entwined branches. There were also numerous wild animals which fell upon the people, especially the children when they wandered too far from their parents while they were playing. So everyone lived in constant fear of death and destruction, and a hopeless despair took hold of the hearts of the folk.

Continuous black darkness had strangled all the light in their hearts. They could not love one another any more. They even hated and murdered one another in their rage. Yet they were forced to remain together, for it was impossible for any single man to defend himself against the attacks of the wild beasts. They had lost all hope of ever finding their way out of the forest. Many of the young people refused to believe in the light they had never seen, and they mocked their elders, when, with a last weak light gleaming in their dim eyes, they recounted tales of the festive, sunny days of their youth.

Among the people, however, there was a young man called Heliopher. He was very much alone, grieving over the misery of his people and seeking a way of salvation. He bore in his heart an endless longing for light and love in the desolation which surrounded him. Heliopher left his people to seek the sun. For many months and years he wandered through the dangers of the forest and of his own soul, and often, very often, nearly lost all hope and confidence. But Heliopher bravely withstood his enemies, whether within himself or around him, and at last he

This story, first published in Plough's *Winter 1938 issue, is based on Maxim Gorky's story "The Flaming Heart of Danko."*

reached the edge of the forest and saw the light of the sun. In terrible amazement he fell into a swoon, and when he awoke he saw in the twilight that he was watched over in his slumber by beautiful people. In the green meadows stood the simple huts of the sun-people, and Heliopher lived with them in peace and endless joy as the most beloved amongst them.

Then Heliopher went back to the forest to seek his people. "Come, brothers and sisters," he said to them, "I will lead you to the light." At this there was murmuring and frowning, wavering and hesitation, wonder and questioning, incredulous laughter, and finally a jubilant "Yes!" And then, at last, the longed-for departure.

Then the light of the sun shone in Heliopher's eyes, but the way was long and difficult, and demanded much suffering and sacrifice, and murmuring arose among the people. Some spoke and said, "Let us murder him, the betrayer of the people!" And the dark glow of hatred was in their eyes. Others were wiser and said, "No! Let us judge him in the presence of all, for it is dangerous to give the people a martyr." And Heliopher spoke to his people, and talked about light and love. But the wise ones answered, "You lie! There is no light, there is no sun, there is no love. Let us be darker than the forest and more cruel than the wild beasts. Then we shall be masters of the forest!"

Heliopher answered in great pain, "O believe not, ye wise men, that ye can be victorious over darkness by being more dark, that ye can overcome the wild beasts by being more beastly. Only love is stronger. Only the light of the sun can drive away darkness."

"Be silent!" said the wise men. "There is no light, there is no sun!"

And the people shouted, flinging their arms about in raging despair, "There is no light, there is no sun!"

But Heliopher called out, "Follow me!" And with his nails he tore open his breast, and his heart burned with love, and it glowed and shed its beams through the dark forest. Then he took it in both hands, held it high over his head, and strode forth in front of the people.

In reverent wonder and silence the multitude followed the burning heart.

And the people went in jubilation toward the sun and danced in its loving rays, and they loved one another. But Heliopher knelt down at the edge of the forest, and with the last strength of his outstretched arms he held up his loving, pulsing heart to the light of heaven, and gave his last smile to his people. ➤

STAUGHTON LYND

The Face *of* Nonviolence *in a* Violent Century

The hundred years from 1914 – when the first shots of World War I rang out – until Israel's invasion of Gaza in 2014 constituted the most violent century in history. Carnage included the Holocaust and ranged from cavalry charges to atomic bombs, with more than 180 million people dying in wartime, according to David Hartsough's estimate in *Waging Peace.* But this bloody century will also be remembered for prophetic lives – such as Mohandas Gandhi, Martin Luther King Jr., and Oscar Romero – who embraced nonviolence, whether as a means of protest or to exemplify the coming kingdom of God.

What does it mean to advocate nonviolence? Pope Francis says that when we renounce violence, we must also "say 'thou shalt not' to an economy of exclusion and inequality. Such an economy kills." In *Evangelii Gaudium* he writes: "How can it be that it is not a news item when an elderly homeless person dies of exposure, but it is news when the stock market loses two points? This is a case of exclusion. Can we continue to stand by when food is thrown away while people are starving? This is a case of

Books discussed in this review:

Worth Fighting For
An Army Ranger's Journey
Out of the Military
and Across America
Rory Fanning
(Haymarket Books)

The Burglary
The Discovery of J. Edgar
Hoover's Secret FBI
Betty Medsger
(Vintage)

It Runs in the Family
On Being Raised by Radicals
and Growing into Rebellious
Motherhood
Frida Berrigan
(OR Books)

Waging Peace
Global Adventures of
a Lifelong Activist
David Hartsough
(PM Press)

From Yale to Jail
The Life Story of a Moral
Dissenter
David Dellinger
(Pantheon Books)

Nonviolence in America
A Documentary History
Staughton and Alice Lynd (ed.)
(Orbis Books)

inequality. . . . [U]ntil exclusion and inequality in society and between peoples is reversed, it will be impossible to eliminate violence."

Historically, the nonviolent way of life has taken a variety of forms, including conscientious objection to military service, intentional communities and alternative living, and nonviolent activism. Each of these remains vital today.

Conscientious Objection

When World War I began, federal law permitted military exemption only to men who could demonstrate conscientious objection to *all* wars on the basis of religious training and belief. Only members of certain well-recognized Christian peace churches, such as Quakers and Mennonites, were permitted civilian alternative service.

Of approximately three thousand prisoners at Fort Leavenworth, Kansas, in 1918, about three hundred were men whose conscientious objection to war had not been recognized by the government. Among them, two Hutterites, Joseph and Michael Hofer, died after being chained to the bars of their cells [see *Plough's* Summer 2014 issue]. Hundreds of other

---

Staughton Lynd is a conscientious objector and civil rights activist; he and his wife Alice, both attorneys, have advocated for Ohio steelworkers, the disabled, and prisoners.

prisoners spontaneously walked off work in protest, a story told in the book *Nonviolence in America,* a collection that my wife and I edited. In every wing of the prison, inmates elected one of their number to serve on a general strike committee. A reporter who happened to be present witnessed the action as it unfolded in the seventh wing. A conscientious objector named Simmons mounted a box.

> He declared that no authority could withstand the power of a united body of men. . . . "Violence accomplishes nothing," [Simmons said]. "Solidarity accomplishes all things. The watchword of the working men throughout the world today is solidarity. Say nothing, do nothing, but stand like this." The speaker folded his arms.

Colonel Rice, the officer in charge, took the prison inmates' demands to Washington, DC. Upon his return, 60 percent of the conscientious objectors had their sentences reduced, and 33 percent were released immediately.

Resisters to military service during World War II included many now known for their leadership in postwar struggles for civil rights and peace. Among them were Bayard Rustin, organizer of the 1963 March on Washington (at which Martin Luther King Jr. gave his "I Have a Dream" speech), and David Dellinger.

Dellinger – who recounts the story in his gripping autobiography *From Yale to Jail* – was imprisoned twice for his refusal to register for the draft. His first prison term was served at Danbury, Connecticut. Here he requested that guards use his name as well as his number when addressing him, and refused to remake his bed on command ("I was the one who slept in it"). He spent a good deal of time in the "hole," that is, solitary confinement.

When convicted the second time, Dellinger was sent to a notorious prison in Lewisburg, Pennsylvania. Here he joined a hunger strike with two objectives: to stop prisoners from being put in the hole and to end censorship of mail. At one point, the prison warden told Dellinger that his wife wanted him to stop his hunger strike – and that she was dying from pregnancy complications. Shaken, he asked to be brought to her. The warden refused. "[T]he more I thought about it," Dellinger wrote, "the more I thought that he had lied to me." He had. Weeks later the men ended their hunger strike after they won on the question of censorship, and Dellinger received a pile of supportive letters from his wife.

Living Out an Alternative

Military conscription during both World Wars had forced thousands of young men throughout the United States to think about their personal responsibility to society. When conscientious objectors were released from Civilian Public Service camps or prison after 1945, many sought positive peacetime alternatives to the root causes of war. They had said "no" to conscription and now yearned for something to say "yes" to. They hoped to discover and pursue a consistently nonviolent way of life.

Some formed intentional communities where economic resources were shared and decision-making was by consensus. My wife and I lived for three years in one such attempt, the Macedonia Cooperative Community in Clarkesville, Georgia. David Hartsough grew up in a similar community, Tanguy Homesteads in Pennsylvania, and describes the experience warmly in his memoir *Waging Peace*: "Moving there was one of the best decisions my parents ever made."

Among pilgrims who have embarked on a more individual quest for peace, one of the most moving is Rory Fanning, who literally walked across the United States. Shortly after 9/11, Rory had volunteered for the Army Rangers. As his belief in nonviolence gradually crystallized, he was befriended by two brothers and fellow Rangers, Pat and Kevin Tillman. Pat Tillman was known to the world as the professional football player who, after the Twin Towers attack and at the height of his career, gave up millions of dollars to volunteer for military service. Pat Tillman was also, according to Fanning, "the first person to suggest to me that it was possible to stand up to the US military. . . . I am alive today, or at least less damaged, because of Pat Tillman."

Margaret Rankin, *Windswept Tree*

As he walked, Fanning carried a heavy pack and a sign that read: "Rory Fanning, who served in the Second Army Ranger Battalion with Pat Tillman, is walking from the Atlantic to the Pacific to raise money for the Pat Tillman Foundation." Everywhere he was befriended and helped.

Reading Fanning's book, *Worth Fighting For,* I was confused at first. There was and is an enormous scandal about Pat Tillman, who was killed in April 2004 in Afghanistan by "friendly fire," that is, by American soldiers. At first, military sources offered the media a concocted story of heroism in the face of the enemy; Tillman's brother and mother later exposed the lie. Why didn't Fanning's sign do likewise?

Gradually I began to understand. When Fanning made known to his Ranger superiors that he had become a conscientious objector, officers went out of their way to disgrace and humiliate him. Regulations require that a soldier who claims conscientious objector status must be given noncombatant assignments until the claim is decided. In Fanning's case, he was sent to the Afghan mountains with his unit. He spent his days chopping firewood. No one spoke to him. No place to sleep was provided him and he had to bed down "outside, often in the snow and the mud, by myself with a single blanket."

Finally his discharge as a CO was approved. Fanning came home feeling he had let his country down by quitting the military. He decided to walk across the country because he was feeling "guilt, betrayal, a sense of adventure, ignorance, a desire to be accepted, pride. . . ." Knowing Pat Tillman was his most positive recent experience. He would walk into towns where he knew no one, protected by Pat.

Is this nonviolence? I say yes. It is recognizing one's vulnerability and, donning that vulnerability, confronting the world exposed and unarmed.

Peaceful Activism

Others pursued nonviolent civil disobedience. Not surprisingly, political activism comes at a cost to one's personal comfort. But what if one's effort to be responsible to the wider human family appears to risk the well-being of one's own spouse, children, or elderly parents? Many activists struggle with such conflicting loyalties.

Perhaps that is why the individuals who broke into an FBI office in Media, Pennsylvania, and revealed the existence of COINTELPRO kept their identities secret for forty years, as recounted in Betty Medsger's excellent book *The Burglary*. Bonnie and John Raines, two of the Media burglars, "revealed their big secret to each of their children separately" long after the fact. When questioned, Bonnie and John explained arrangements they had made for their family to be raised by Bonnie's parents and uncle had they – Bonnie and John – been imprisoned. But the difficult question remained: "How could they have cared so deeply about anything that they were willing to risk having the family severed?"

Frida Berrigan addresses this question in her memoir *It Runs in the Family*. She is the daughter of the late Philip Berrigan and Elizabeth McAlister, former priest and nun. Prison separated her parents for eleven of their twenty-nine years of marriage. Although her father and mother tried to avoid being incarcerated at the same time, Frida said she "turned three and my brother turned two while they were away. We all struggled with being apart."

Parents can never know with certainty how their nonviolent activism will affect their children. When I left home to make an unauthorized trip to Hanoi in December 1965, my seven-year-old son Lee clung to my legs, trying to stop me. As it turned out, I was not imprisoned upon returning; Lee, now fifty-six, and I, at eighty-five, are both doing well.

Because the intensity of my objection to the Vietnam War caused me to be expelled from academia, I came to know displaced steelworkers and high-security prisoners. My wife and I found our way to what Archbishop Romero called "accompaniment." We went to law school, acquired a skill that steelworkers and prisoners desperately needed, and as attorneys were privileged – are privileged – to walk beside certain of the poor and oppressed.

I believe this is the form of activism the world most needs. We do not presume to provide strategy from on high. The chairs are in a circle, and we learn as well as teach.

A Surprising Power

From the books under review, the nonviolent action that impressed me most deeply is told in Medsger's book, *The Burglary*. During the summer of 1971 a group of war-resisters planned to raid the Selective Service office in Camden, New Jersey, to destroy draft records as a statement against the ongoing war in Vietnam. One of their number, Robert Hardy, secretly agreed to be an informant for the FBI. The group was apprehended after they broke into the Camden office and faced possible prison sentences of more than forty years.

While trial preparations were underway, Hardy's nine-year-old son Billy died tragically in an accident. Father Michael Doyle, one of the defendants, had been a longtime family friend and conducted Billy's funeral; in church, "the FBI agents and the people they had arrested were sitting near each other." After the funeral, "Peg and Bob Hardy showed Doyle two pieces of wood they had found in Billy's dresser drawer. With a nail and hammer Billy had chiseled the word 'peace' in one and the word 'love' in the other."

Billy's sudden death impacted the trial that followed. Billy's father, Robert Hardy, became a witness for the defense. All twenty-eight defendants were acquitted.

This story illustrates why nonviolence is best described as a belief that love will find a way – or, as Quakers say, that "way will open." When way opens, it may not be because we sought it or made it happen. Way must open between nuclear-armed nation-states as it did in the Cuban Missile Crisis. Way can open between heavily armed guardians of authority and unarmed protesters. Again and again, when it looks least likely, way will open. ⭜

The Buried Giant: A Novel
Kazuo Ishiguro (Knopf)

In the Britain of Ishiguro's mythic tale, grass grows on Roman ruins, Britons and Saxons share an uneasy peace, and a wanderer might still cross paths with an ogre or dragon. A spell of forgetfulness seems to envelop the country like fog. An elderly couple, Axl and Beatrice, set out from their village to find their son and recover their lost memories. Will they break the spell, or are some things best left unremembered – especially in the wake of wholesale slaughter? Throughout the ensuing drama, the tender love Axl and Beatrice share shines like a jewel. Can it survive if the buried giant of their forgotten past reawakens?

Ancient Christian Worship
Andrew B. McGowan (Baker)

How did the first Christians worship? The New Testament tells us they gathered daily to pray, sing, and share meals. McGowan fleshes out this picture using other early sources to show how much of the rich diversity of Christian worship today – singing, dancing, praying, baptizing, anointing, teaching, preaching, prophesying, feasting, and fasting – has its roots in the first through fourth centuries. When did Sunday church services start? What about Christmas? Why did many early Christians pray five times a day? This thorough, authoritative work gives a challenging glimpse into the lives of our forerunners in the faith.

Scavenger Loop: Poems
David Baker (Norton)

The masterful thirty-page title poem has it all: a whirlwind of poetic forms, our tempestuous love affair with nature, lost innocence, a dying mother, materialism, GM corn, trash pickers, and our inevitable return to dust. Baker, poetry editor of the *Kenyon Review*, rarely fails to bring us back down to earth: ". . . I've read / the dust of long-blown stars seeds empty / space. / *Go get your saw*, he says. *I'll grab my*

gloves." Though the shadow of loss, absence, and regret falls across many of these poems, it doesn't dampen the poet's obvious love for his language and his land. In "Heaven" all it takes is a cicada:

I don't know what has shocked me more,
that you are gone, that I am still here,
that there is music after the end.

See the author's poem "Errand" on page 23.

Where the Cross Meets the Street
Noel Castellanos (IVP Books)

In this spiritual memoir, Castellanos, who leads the Christian Community Development Association and has written on immigration for *Plough,* takes us back to his roots in a Mexican farmworker family in Texas. He honors those who helped form him – a fifth grade teacher who believed in him, a football coach who brought him to Jesus – and describes landing in the white, evangelical world of Christian college. Inspired by his mentor John Perkins and by Latin American liberation theologians, he moved to a Chicago barrio with his young family to found a church that confronts injustice and restores community. In his candid description of both the rewards and failures he's experienced, Castellanos shows us why God's love for those at the margins – a love demonstrated on the cross – should be the center of every Christian's life.

The Road to Character
David Brooks (Random House)

A leading pundit, Brooks confesses that in his rise to fame he's neglected certain fundamentals. Like many ambitious souls, he has focused on "resumé virtues" instead of "eulogy virtues": courage, kindness, honesty, generosity, depth of character. These are traits shared by the "deeply good" people whom we all want to resemble. Though Brooks's moral vision blurs at times (don't "follow your heart" into adultery, for instance), we're heartened that a bestseller is pointing so many people in the right direction. ➳

The Editors

Everyone Belongs to God

*A leader in the New Monastic movement introduces a
new book on mission by Christoph Friedrich Blumhardt (1842–1919).*

JONATHAN WILSON-HARTGROVE

In every age, God's people need prophets to help us see beyond our blind spots – to expand our vision of what God is about.

Jeremiah was a prophet. To a people in exile, caught between the false hope that their God would destroy Babylon and the despair of thinking God had forgotten them, Jeremiah proclaimed a new vision. The old images of God's faithfulness would no longer suffice. Yes, their God had saved humanity in an ark and washed away the wicked in a great flood. Yes, their God had brought them out of Egypt, drowning Pharaoh's army in the Red Sea.

But a salvation that requires someone else's destruction is too small a salvation, Jeremiah proclaimed. To a people in exile, he wrote, "Seek the peace and prosperity of the city to which I have carried you into exile. Pray to the Lord for it, because if it prospers, you too will prosper" (Jer. 29:7). You will not be saved apart from your neighbors, the prophet says. Everyone belongs to God.

Jesus came preaching peace to all people. But he got into the most trouble for showing the religious insiders how the people they counted out often understood the advent of God's reign better than they did. Take Luke 4. For his first sermon in his own hometown, Jesus took a text from Isaiah, the prophet. And when he said that the great day of Jubilee had arrived for God's people, everyone rejoiced.

But when he pointed out that a Syrian soldier and a Gentile woman had more faith than anyone else in their day, the hometown crowd tried to throw him off a cliff.

Your gospel is too small, Jesus said. But no one wants the prophet to speak so directly to them. Better to celebrate that the scripture is fulfilled in our hearing than to grapple with the ways God's word forces us to expand our imagination.

But expand we must. At least, that's what the prophets tell us.

The text of Blumhardt's *Everyone Belongs to God* (Plough, May 2015) is over a century old,

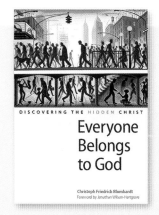

*Everyone Belongs to God:
Discovering the Hidden Christ*
Christoph Friedrich Blumhardt
163 pages, softcover
Plough, 2015

Do we need to make everyone on the planet into Christians?

How can Christians represent the love of Christ to their neighbors (let alone people in foreign countries) in an age when Christianity has earned a bad name from centuries of intolerance and cultural imperialism? This provocative book, based on a recently translated collection of one-hundred-year-old letters from a famous pastor to his son-in-law, a missionary in China, will upend many assumptions about what it means to give witness to Christ.

At a time when Christian mission has too often been reduced to social work or proselytism, this book invites us to reclaim the heart of Jesus' Great Commission, quietly but confidently incarnating the love of Christ and trusting him to do the rest.

but it contains the words of a prophet who was ahead of his time. At the beginning of the so-called "Christian Century," when science and progress seemed to be bringing Christendom to its full height of glory, Christoph Friedrich Blumhardt heard a word that cut through his cultural formation and easy assumptions: Everyone belongs to God.

Cultural captivity is, of course, a far cry from exile, but the long march of Christendom, as we now see more clearly, took God's people as far from the Promised Land as Nebuchadnezzar's forces ever did. As in the Babylonian captivity, we face a dual temptation.

On the one hand, there are those who say, "All you've got to do is believe." God is greater than the forces of secularism and materialism, atheism and individualism. Yes, Western Christianity is compromised. But the pure in heart – those who really believe – can be saved right here, right now. All you have to do is bow your head and say this simple prayer. . . .

On the other hand, the cynics point out, the Good Book became the Bad Book in so much of the Western missionary enterprise. We over-evangelized the world too lightly, exporting cultural hegemony along with the faith, doing more harm than good. Christendom has failed, they say, and so it is best to leave the name of Christ behind. Do good, for goodness' sake. At the very least, try to do no harm.

In the midst of this crisis, I hear Blumhardt's words for twenty-first-century Christians in the same vein as Jeremiah's to seventh-century-BC Israel: "The Risen One wants to draw people to himself, and so propaganda for a particular confession of faith or church is no concern of his. You must stand up and represent the gospel of the kingdom that

> **"In every street and workplace,** it should be proclaimed: 'You all belong to God! Whether you are godless or devout, under judgment or under grace, blessed or damned, you belong to God, and God is good and wants what is best for you. Whether you are dead or alive, righteous or unrighteous, in heaven or in hell, you belong to God, and as soon as you are swept into the current of faith, the good within you will emerge.' Speak like this and you will have different results from those who peddle the truncated gospel that gives with one hand and takes away with the other." ·
>
> **Christoph Friedrich Blumhardt**

shines for all people, no matter who they are."

We cannot give up on the missionary enterprise because we have misunderstood and abused it. Instead, Blumhardt insists, we must reclaim the heart of Christian mission.

Our gospel has been too small. It is, indeed, too small a thing to think that the hope of the world rests in our ability to recruit others into a religion which has too often made us morally worse.

To confess that the hope of the world is Jesus Christ is to open ourselves to a kingdom beyond our control – beyond our imagination, even. It is to embrace the revolutionary notion that everyone belongs to God.

Though Bonhoeffer had not yet introduced the term when Blumhardt wrote these letters, it was in the midst of his own confrontation with the crisis of Western Christianity that he wrote of "religionless Christianity." Bonhoeffer had so little time to explore what this term meant, even less how one might practice it in the world. But this volume fills some of that void. For it, we can all be grateful. Take and read the words of a prophet for our time. ➘

Jonathan Wilson-Hartgrove lives at the Rutba House, a Christian community and house of hospitality in Durham, North Carolina. He is the author of Strangers at My Door *(Convergent, 2013). This article is from the foreword to Blumhardt's* Everyone Belongs to God, *a new book from Plough (see opposite).*

Badshah Khan
and the Servants of God

"**N**onviolence is not for cowards," Mahatma Gandhi told his friend Badshah Khan in 1930. "It is for the brave, the courageous." At the time they were working shoulder to shoulder, a Hindu and a Muslim, for Indian independence and for peace, as described in Eknath Easwaran's biography, *Nonviolent Soldier of Islam* (Nilgiri, 1999).

Khan (1890–1988) was born Abdul Ghaffar Khan near Peshawar, in what is now Pakistan but was then British India's North-West Frontier Province. The region was notorious for the violent uprisings of the Pathans (or Pashtuns), a fiercely proud Muslim people who followed an ancient code of tribal honor that caused fierce family feuds to rage for generations.

> "If you want your people to prosper, you must start living for community."

The son of a prosperous landowner, Khan was educated in missionary schools. He was then offered a commission with the Guides, an elite military corps, but turned it down. He increasingly turned his attention to the uneducated, impoverished people of his region, traveling from village to village, building schools, and teaching about agriculture and sanitation. His organizing work earned him the attention of the British who, worried about the burgeoning Free India movement, were suspicious of any attempts to unite the Pathans.

Khan was arrested in 1921 as a subversive, and remained imprisoned until 1924. After his release, he established a nonviolent army called the Khudai Khidmatgars ("Servants of God"). Organized with the structure of a professional military force, it was open to all Pathans, both women and men, who were willing to take its oath of service and nonviolence. Known as the Red Shirts for the color of their uniform, Khudai Khidmatgars announced that "freedom is our goal" – freedom from British oppression, from poverty and ignorance, and from the violence of their own culture. They opened schools, taught, and organized public meetings. Khan insisted that women be allowed an education. He said in a speech: "God makes no distinction between men and women. If someone can surpass another, it is only through good deeds and morals."

Despite their nonviolence, the Khudai Khidmatgars faced some of the harshest repression meted out by British troops to any independence group. In an April 1930 massacre in Peshawar, the group's unarmed members faced sustained machine-gun fire, and at least two hundred were killed. Witnesses reported that they went willingly and nonviolently to their deaths, clutching only their Qurans and shouting, "God is great!"

When independence finally arrived in 1947, Khan opposed the All-India Muslim League's demand for the partition of Pakistan and India, earning the enmity of Pakistan's first leader, Muhammad Ali Jinnah. Khan was placed under house arrest until 1954, and was repeatedly imprisoned in the 1960s and 1970s. He died under house arrest in 1988, having spent a total of thirty years in confinement.

Khan's legacy continues to inspire new generations of nonviolent Muslim activists – such as Nobel Peace Prize laureate Malala Yousafzai – who bear out Khan's words: "That person is a Muslim who never hurts anyone by word or deed, but who works for the benefit and happiness of God's creatures." ➤ *Veery Huleatt*